BUDGETING

FOR BEGINNERS

How to Save Money and Manage Your Finances
With a Personal Budget Plan

(Learn How to Manage Your Finances and Start
Saving Now)

Lorraine McKinney

Published by Alex Howard

Lorraine McKinney

Budgeting for Beginners: How to Save Money and Manage Your Finances With a Personal Budget Plan (Learn How to Manage Your Finances and Start Saving Now)

ISBN 978-1-77485-063-3

Legal & Disclaimer

The information contained in this book is not designed to replace or take the place of any form of medicine or professional medical advice. The information in this book has been provided for educational and entertainment purposes only.

The information contained in this book has been compiled from sources deemed reliable, and it is accurate to the best of the Author's knowledge; however, the Author cannot guarantee its accuracy and validity and cannot be held liable for any errors or omissions. Changes are periodically made to this book. You must consult your doctor or get professional medical advice before using any of the suggested remedies, techniques, or information in this book.

Table of Contents

Introduction

This book has eye opening information on how to take advantage of the limitless wealth building power of the compound effect.

The regular person goes through grade school and high school, graduates with a high school diploma, and then goes to college. He or she takes out large loan amounts to foot college tuition and other bills. By the time the regular person completes college, he or she is $50,000 in debt.

Just like that, the fellow applies for a job, gets it, and perhaps embarks on following the example set by parents and other adults: paying off multiple bills, plus the outstanding loan immediately the paycheck comes in, and following this up with paying off multiple credit card charges accrued over the month. Once this happens, the credit card abuse pattern repeats with the result being an unappealing paycheck-to-paycheck living with nothing saved up. By the time retirement rolls around, the next step is surely death since any financial plan created was a haste decision, and is thus too thin to promise comfort.

Such a life is a bleak one, one you would not wish upon your enemy. Why wish it on yourself? Lucky for you, with this book by your side, you don't have to let your life follow this path.

This book discusses financial nuggets that will help you develop financial smartness from a youthful age. By the way, it is not normal for us to have financially disorganized lives all our lives. The reason why this seems so common is that most of us make poor day-to-day financial decisions.

With the information and tips discussed in this guide, you can play a different ball game so that you and yours never have to want for money. Everything you learn in this book will help you to understand why compounding is the best thing that happened, especially because it allows even the ordinary Joe who never earned a lot of money in his working life to build a life that some people who had high flying careers and successful businesses can only dream about in their sunset years. With this book, you will unlock to secret to wealth building and how to make the most of this secret i.e. compound interest, to your benefit.

Let's begin!

Thanks again for downloading this book. I hope you enjoy it!

Chapter 1: Back To The Basics

A budget is simply a spending plan; it is a strategy that you put in place to basically 'tell' your money what to do every month. In your budget, you list all your sources of income and allocate that money to varied expenditures.

Having such a detailed budget is important as it will enable you to make smarter decisions with your income every day. In a situation where you want to spend money on something, a budget will require you to stop and think about the money you are about to spend on a particular item or service, and really question whether what you want to spend money on is necessary.

Despite a budget being an amazing financial tool and something that we all should strive to have, for most people, budgeting does not ring as something great. Most people view budgeting as a way of depriving themselves, as is the case of a healthy diet. Unfortunately, when you have such a mindset, you will avoid preparing a budget just as you avoid dieting. On the contrary, just as a diet is a plan for how you eat, budgeting is a plan for how you spend.

Other people think that budgeting is only for those who are beginning to run low on cash. For example, many university students tend to draft personal budgets to work out how they can make ends meet due to their limited incomes and high expenses. The truth of the matter is that budgeting should not only be useful as an option when your finances are dwindling or when you're going through a major transition in your life.

The budgeting process is for everyone, for the poor and rich alike. In fact, proper budgeting could make you rich. Just look at a company the size of Amazon. Do you think they would be where they are at the moment without good budgeting? Even some of the wealthiest people have accrued fortunes as a result of proper budgeting. Warren Buffet is the perfect example. There is no way that he or his company Berkshire Hathaway could enjoy so much success without focusing on all details about their quarterly, monthly or annual outflow and inflow. This shows that budgeting can not only get you out of a rut; it could also help you secure your financial success.

I believe you have a better understanding of budgeting now. Before we get started on steps to take to come up with a suitable budget, let us look at some of the excuses you may have about budgeting. Evaluating these excuses will enable you to understand where you are coming from and find ways of dealing with these excuses because they could be what is holding you back from taking the plunge.

Chapter 2: Budgeting Fundamentals

Your budgeting plan should be simple. In the beginning, most people feel stressed when budgeting. The process of resisting urges and old habits can be exhausting. A complicated budgeting plan will only confuse you. This will add more challenges to your already stressful financial life. In this chapter, we will discuss the basic process of budgeting. We will elaborate on each part of the process of succeeding chapters.

Budgeting Fundamental #1: Start with a goal

You should always have financial goals. Some financial goals are obvious. Everyone around us saves for a house, the kids' college fund, or for retirement, so we should do the same. Aside from these default financial goals, however, most people are confused with what they want to save for. We will discuss how you can arrive at a worthwhile financial goal later on. For now, you should think of the things or achievements that will make you genuinely happy. All your financial goals should lead to your happiness. It may also lead to the happiness of the people around you. If they do not, you will be working and sacrificing for nothing.

The planning stage

The next step is to develop a plan that will bring us closer to our goals. You can use the strategies in this book to start your budget planning. Most of the time, we already know what we need to do to be able to save money for our goals. However, because we do not put it in writing, we never get to apply our knowledge.

Planning organizes our ideas so that we can have a clear picture of what we need to do. Our plan should guide us in our daily financial decisions so that all our financial activities support the completion of our goals.

Time for Action

After planning, we need to make sure that we put our plan into action. The ideal scenario is that we will do exactly what is written in our plans. Old habits and urges to spend will challenge our abilities to put the plan into action. Your ability to resist them is crucial to the success of your plan.

Everything in moderation

Budgeting prevents us from spending too much on something. Our budget planning will only be successful if we do everything in moderation. Let's take drinking for example. Most adults drink. Most drinkers practice it in moderation. However, there are those who overdo drinking. The constant visits to the pub make them spend more on alcoholic beverages than the average person does. Because of drinking's many biological effects, the alcoholic's productivity and overall self-control are also affected. The disturbance in his productivity may affect his income while his lack of self-control when he is drunk may lead to more unnecessary expenses. The same pattern happens with all addictive habits.

When budgeting, you aim to keep your spending in each aspect of life in moderation. You need to become accustomed to regular priced items rather than their expensive counterparts. If you want to be efficient in the ways you spend your money; you should also avoid expensive brands. Buying expensive brands is only acceptable if they provide exceptional quality and if they will last longer than their less expensive counterparts.

100% Awareness

We can only practice moderation in all aspects of life if we are constantly aware of how we use our money. You need to know how much money you have in all your accounts at all times. In the chapters that follow, we will discuss the multiple tools that you can use to be constantly aware of your finances. By being aware of your spending, you will know if you are following the budgeting plan or if you are deviating from it.

This is where most people fail when budgeting. They make a great budget plan, and they try to implement it. At the beginning of the process, their awareness of their expenses is at its peak. After a while, however, they become bored of the plan. They begin to become less interested in their expenses. Their awareness level begins to go down. When this happens, the budgeter may fail to take note of some expenses. This will lead to some inefficient spending practices. The accumulation of bad spending practices will decrease the likelihood that the goal will be reached.

As soon as you start implementing your budget plan, you need to make sure that you have 100% awareness of your spending habits. We will discuss how you can achieve this in future chapters.

Performance analysis and budgeting remedies

You need to analyze your expense records to see if you are getting closer to your goals. You will not be able to implement your plan to perfection on your first try. In the beginning, habits developed in the past will severely affect your performance. If you have 100% awareness of your spending activities, you will be able to identify which habits cause the most financial damage.

When you identify these problem areas, the next step is to find remedies that will stop the financial bleeding. You should then insert these remedies into your plan as you revise it.

Common Motivation for Budgeting

Budgeting can be challenging if you have not developed it into a habit. You need to make hard choices every day to implement your plan properly. You will be declining offers from friends to eat out or to buy more than one bottle of beer after work. The hardest challenge of all is to resist old habits that may be causing our financial problems.

In the beginning, you need to find ways to motivate yourself into budgeting. You need to have an excellent reason to save money. Most parents work hard and sacrifice their immediate gratifications for their children. Some people save up to fund continuing education. You should think of your reason for becoming efficient with your money.

You need to examine your situation and ask yourself why you need to start budgeting. Here are some reasons that may motivate you to start this habit.

You will be able to save for great experiences

By budgeting every day, your family will be able to save for things that you normally would not be able to afford. If you know how to follow a budget plan, you will be able to save money that you can use for giving great experiences to your kids.

You will be prepared for all expenses, expected or not

Budgeting allows you to save a part of your money for the future. You will be able to save for all your financial goals given enough time. For the unexpected goals, you have an emergency fund. You will also avail of services that will prepare you for possible emergencies like accidents and hospitalization.

You will be able to prevent bad financial practices that may destroy your future

One of the key principles of budgeting is constant awareness of where your money is going. In the steps to creating your budgeting system, you will be instructed to take note of all your expenses. By keeping track of all your expenses, you will be able to examine your past expenses. You will be able to identify categories of expenses that hurt your financial life the most. When you have identified them, you will be able to prevent these bad spending activities from becoming habits.

It will keep your family happy and contented

A family that budgets is happier and more contented with life. An effective budgeter is always ahead in paying his bills. He does not react towards expenses. He tries to anticipate them and implement strategies to deal with them even when the deadline is still far. If you deal with expenses this way, life will be a lot less stressful.

You will be able to teach your children how to of budget, save and reach their financial goals

If you practice budgeting consistently, you will be able to teach your children the financial principles that you follow by being a good example to them. You will be able to show them the importance of delayed gratification.

If you want them to learn how to budget properly, you should teach them the process of budgeting. You should also make them aware of the common bad spending practices that may prevent them from implementing their budget plan properly. You should make them focus on the family's goals. You should also show consistency when practicing your budgeting plan, especially when spending in front of your children. If your children see that budgeting can be done successfully, they will be more confident with their money management skills when they become adults.

Chapter 3: How Can I Manage My Finances Better

A great portion of American citizens doesn't nicely manipulate their money. Some sources file that Americans are quite awful on the subject of their finance compared to different advanced nations.

But, there may be a desire for you if you locate yourself amongst this group.

There are some brilliant attempted-and-tested strategies you could learn how to manage your cash properly.

Having a legitimate money management plan can be the light at the cease of the tunnel for people looking to get their monetary existence so as.

If you are like me and feature several bank money owed, credit score cards, an IRA, and so forth, regularly times getting a grip and completely information your private finance country would possibly seem daunting and an uphill war.

But if you don't take the right steps to get organized and in reality study approaches for better dealing with your price range, you'll sense like you are swimming towards the cutting-edge.

Dealing with your money—like whatever—takes time to apprehend and to improve on. And to master, it additionally takes dedication and a solid understanding of your monetary state of affairs. These are the first steps in effective money management.

Anybody and everybody who ever took manage in their finances went via this, and getting your monetary existence in order, faster in place of later, is of maximum importance.

Here are 10 fundamental steps to help you manipulate your cash the right manner:

1. Create a budget

First matters first: create a budget if you haven't already. Is it important? Are our windshield wipers necessary within the rain? Consider me, you need one.

Growing and sticking to a finance would possibly appear a bit hard to reap at the start however it will pay off in the end (no pun supposed). Budgeting enables us to see with clarity and complete transparency our economic scenario and this is of the maximum significance for higher managing your money.

It's the first step to assist us to pay off debt and start saving for future fees such as a loan, a car, and your retirement. It's what is going to convey balance in your financial lifestyles and provide you with peace of thought.

To begin, you may want to recognize your charges and your profits to better control your money. That is addressed inside the following 2 steps:

2. Recognize your fees

Ask everyone off the pinnacle of their head to inform you the way lots they spend a month on the entirety and they might not be able to accomplish that. This isn't uncommon.

Many people sincerely don't realize the whole amount of costs they generate on any given month. That is a hassle however there may be a smooth solution for it. Right here it's miles: for one month, preserve song of all your costs. Easy-peasy. Take all your receipts (groceries, restaurant payments, utilities, and many others.) and have a look at your financial institution statements and add up all of your prices. Consider keeping track of prices paid using cash as well as credit score playing cards.

The concept is to have all of your costs (each variable and stuck) accounted for to get a total quantity. This will let you see the whole picture and realize the way to manipulate your prices going forward. You may additionally need to examine your historic overall performance over the years.

3. Understand your income

That is the distinction between earnings and prices, the majority realize their complete monthly profits however have less know-how of their complete month-to-month expenses.

Nevertheless, the point is to discern your overall costs and subtract that from your total earnings for the month in question. Here is how the effects ought to pan out:

If you grow to be with a wonderful number this is good (excessive 5!) and way you spent much less you made. You may grow your debt payments or boom your financial savings.

After you understand your expenses and earnings and have firm information about the cash coming inside and out of your lifestyles, it's time to take some extra steps to satisfactory control your cash.

4. Consolidate your debt

The primary factor to do is to get it underneath manipulate and paintings on doing away with it. If you have credit score card money owed, student loans, and other debts; appearance to consolidate them and attempt to get the lowest interest charge viable.

Again, it's all approximately taking the proper steps to control your cash. There are alternatives accessible that assist you to integrate several unsecured money owed together with credit playing cards, private loans, and payday loans, into one bill in place of paying them in my opinion.

If you most effectively have an unmarried credit card debt and are on a tight price range, strive to pay at least the minimum quantity as quickly as you get the credit score card bill. Then, if your budget allows it, and you come across a few more money, try and make the same fee a few weeks later.

Attempt preserving this fee cycle going till your debt is fully paid off.

5. Slash or cast off unnecessary expenses

If you are buying a Venti Caffe Latte every day (as delicious as they are) that's around $four from your pockets. Multiply that out and you may be spending approximately $1,400 a year just on that. Maybe, just perhaps, keep in mind making your blend at home to pinch those pennies?

Paying for a health club but doing yoga in your backyard? Cancel it. Suppose long and tough of different memberships, subscriptions, money owed that you are paying for but may want to live without.

Recollect, the idea is to discover ways to manipulate your budget better by utilizing taking the whole lot and every penny into consideration.

So, do a little spring cleansing and decrease charges wherever you notice a possibility and specifically if it's something that doesn't affect your lifestyles to a splendid volume.

6. Create an emergency fund

It's properly to be organized. Emergency finance is a vital part of a healthful personal finance plan.

In nearly all instances, you shouldn't touch or take money out of the fund, alternatively, permit it to sit down there earning hobby. If you lose your process or an unlucky or sudden fee arises— consisting of your automobile breaking down or a tree falling to your roof—this is while you must faucet into it.

7. Store 10 to 15 percent for retirement

I realize it's a way off, however, if you need to be sipping margaritas in Miami below a solar umbrella, the sooner you begin saving for retirement, the better off you will be on your golden years.

The first component ought to be to set up a financial savings target—one which tells you about how a lot you have to set aside over the years to satisfy your retirement desires to will let you stay the type of way of life you envision.

You are 21 years vintage and don't have anything saved up but just got supplied a task paying $40,000 in 12 months. If you shop 10% of your earnings annually then using the retirement age of 67, you'll have $2.Five million saved up!

If you need a calculator to run your numbers, check this one out.

8. Assessment and apprehend your credit score report

Why are credit score reports so crucial?

A credit document is a number roughly between a hundred and fifty and 900 that serves as a score/grade which elements on your present and past loans, credit score cards, mortgages, and every other suggested money owed.

It serves to determine how creditworthy you're and this rating has a right away effect to your future borrowing capacity. It's essential which you review and understand your credit score report to assure it has all of your up to date records and to pick out any viable errors (it's anticipated that 2-3% of reports include some errors that would affect your normal rating).

If you want to aim for a high-quality credit score rating, keep your credit score card balances low and work on paying off your debt instead of moving it from account to account.

9. Use a tool or personal financial finance app

Your budget is already complex, shall we clear-cut them.

How?

Start through getting with the times and placing away your abacus or Casio calculator. There is new and free equipment obtainable to be able to display your approaches to control cash as well as do all of the tough budgeting and computational paintings.

Many mechanisms which include Quicken for windows or the loose Money Strands app will let you appropriately consolidate, control and control your money multi-functional region.

With Money Strands, you could get access to all your account balances, financial transactions, spending conduct and budgets, and take all that records to begin making smarter choices and acquire your financial desires.

10. Comply with cash control sources

Information is energy. Every financial guru we understand nowadays began off such as you and me. They just constantly learned and educated themselves and grew to become their ardor into their profession.

Monetary pros can give you some great deal-wanted advice on the way to manipulate your coins the right manner, as well as a few inspiring tales to get you focused on being the high-quality version of yourself in terms of crushing it financially.

The important thing when learning which expert to comply with is to cautiously take note of what they are saying, take in it, and handiest take the portions of recommendation or steerage that may without a doubt assist your case.

A number of their financial jargon might be from your league, so appearance extra for those kernels of information that would apply to you and yours.

Normal, live well-informed, exercise sound financial management, and possibly someday you will be the following personal finance guru and feature thousands, if not thousands and thousands, of human beings sharing your content material and searching for your information on the pleasant way to manage your money. Anything is possible.

Being able to efficiently control your cash will make existence glide a whole lot greater easily, not to mention help decrease your pressure tiers. Being properly-organized will even save you time and prevent complications in the future. And no one needs the ones.

So, get available and take the first steps mapping out your personal financial approach with the ever-present aim in mind of being capable of control your budget better than before. Many others have performed it and so can you.

Simple Ways to Manage Your Money Better

Being accurate with cash is set more than just making ends meet. Do not worry that you're no longer a math whiz; extremely good math competencies are not important - you want to recognize fundamental addition and subtraction.

Lifestyles are a good deal less difficult when you have accurate monetary capabilities. The way you spend your money affects your credit score score and the amount of debt you emerge as wearing. If you're suffering from money control, as an example, you're dwelling paycheck to paycheck no matter making more than sufficient money; here are a few suggestions to improve your financial habits.

While you're faced with a spending choice, particularly a huge buy choice, don't just anticipate you can have enough money something. Affirm that you could honestly have the funds for it and which you haven't already committed those funds to another expense.

A way to manipulate your money better

Have a budget: Many humans don't finance due to the fact they don't want to go through what they suppose can be a monotonous process of listing out fees, including up numbers, and making sure everything strains up. If you're bad with money, you don't have room for excuses with budgeting. If all it takes to get your spending on course is some hours operating a budget each month, why wouldn't you do it? As opposed to focusing on the technique of creating a budget, recognition on the fee that budgeting will carry in your lifestyles.

Song Your Spending: Small purchases right here and there adds up quickly, and before you comprehend it, you've overspent your finances. Begin monitoring your spending to find out places where you may be unknowingly overspending. Keep your receipts and write your purchases in a spending journal, categorizing them so that you can become aware of areas where you have got a hard time preserving your spending in taking a look at.

Don't commit to Any New habitual monthly bills: just due to the fact your earnings and credit qualify you for a positive mortgage, it doesn't mean you should take it. Many people naively suppose the bank wouldn't approve them for a credit score card or mortgage they couldn't afford. The bank handiest is aware of your profits, as you've stated, and the debt duties covered to your credit document, no longer another obligation that would save you you from making your bills on time. It's up to you to determine whether a month-to-month fee is cheap based totally for your earnings and different monthly responsibilities.

Ensure You're Paying the quality prices: you may make the maximum of your money evaluation buying, making sure that you're paying the lowest fees for products and services. Search for reductions, coupons, and cheaper alternatives every time you can.

Store Up for large Purchases: The ability to delay gratification will cross alongside the way in helping you be higher with money. While you eliminate large purchases, rather than sacrificing greater critical necessities or placing the purchase on a credit score card, you supply your self-time to evaluate whether or not the purchase is important and even extra time to compare costs. By saving up as opposed to using a credit score, you keep away from paying a hobby on the purchase. And if you keep in place of skipping payments or obligations, well, you shouldn't cope with the numerous effects of lacking one's bills.

Restrict your credit Card Purchases: credit playing cards are a terrible spender's worst enemy. While you run out of cash, you turn on your credit playing cards without considering whether or not you could find the money to pay the balance. Face up to the urge to use your credit cards for purchases you may have enough money, mainly on items you don't need.

Contribute to financial savings often: Depositing money into a savings account every month assist you to build healthy economic habits. You may even set it up, so the money is robotically transferred out of your bank account in your savings account. That way, you mustn't recall to make the transfer.

Being correct With cash Takes practice: in the start, you can now not be used to making plans in advance and getting rid of purchases till you may have enough money. The more you make those conduct part of your daily lifestyles, the less difficult it's miles to manipulate your cash, and the better off your finance could be.

5 Keys to efficiently dealing with yourPersonal financial budget

Wouldn't or not it's high-quality if there have been a magic method or easy trick that allowed you to by no means must worry approximately money or control your finances once more?

While that may not be realistic, there are a few simple matters you may do proper now to improve your cash state of affairs. Try these 5 steps for efficiently managing your personal financial budget. Another bonus? If you keep on with those 5 recommendations, your financial troubles may additionally begin to diminish, and you can start reaping the rewards of decrease debt, saving for the future, and a stable credit rating.

Detail your financial dreams

Take some time to jot down particular, lengthy-term financial dreams. You can want to take a month-lengthy trip to Europe, purchase investment assets, or retire early. All of those dreams will affect how you plan your price range. As an instance, your aim to retire early is depending on how properly you store your money now. Different desires, inclusive of homeownership, starting a circle of relatives, shifting, or changing careers will all be stricken by the way you manage your price range.

As soon as you've got written down your financial dreams, prioritize them. This ensures which you are paying the maximum attention to those which can be of the highest significance to you. You can additionally list them in the order you want to attain them, however, a protracted-term goal like saving for retirement requires you to paintings towards it while also operating to your other desires.

Beneath are a few suggestions on a way to get clear for your monetary desires:

Set long-term desires like getting out of debt, buying a domestic, or retiring early. These goals are separate from your brief-term desires.

Set short-time period goals, like following a budget, decreasing your spending, paying down or not the usage of your credit scorecards.

Prioritize your dreams to help you create a monetary plan.

Flesh out Your Plan

A monetary plan is important in supporting you attain your economic goals. The plan should have more than one step or milestones. A sample plan might include growing a monthly budget and spending plan, then getting out of debt.

After you've accomplished those three matters and have followed thru on your new plan for a few months, you may locate that you have extra money, and the money you unfastened up from your debt bills may be used to attain your next round of goals.

Again, it is key to determine what priorities are maximum vital to you. Maintain steadily working closer to your lengthy-time period retirement desires, but also begin to awareness on the maximum important close to-term desires you've got set for yourself. Do you want to take an extravagant journey? Begin investing? Purchase a domestic or construct your very own enterprise? These are all matters to recollect when choosing your next step.

Your dreams, alongside an emergency fund, will assist you to stop making monetary choices primarily based on fear and assist you to get control of your situation.

While growing an economic plan, take into account these items:

Your finance is key to achievement. It's miles the tool a good way to give you the maximum manipulate of your monetary destiny. Your finances are the key to achieving the rest of your plan.

You have to preserve contributing to lengthy-time period goals, like saving for retirement, regardless of what degree of your monetary plan you're in.

Constructing an emergency fund is some other key element to economic success and pressure discounts.

Make and persist with finances

Your budget is considered one of the most important gear to help you be triumphant financially. It permits you to create a spending plan so that you can allocate your money in a manner to help you to reach your desires.

You could make your budget as high-degree or distinct as you need, as long as it facilitates you reach your last goal of spending much less than you earn, paying off any debts, padding your emergency fund, and saving for the destiny.

A budget may even assist you to decide how to spend your cash over the approaching months and years. Without the plan, you may spend your coins on matters that seem vital now, however, do not offer a lot in phrases of enhancing your future. Many people get stuck in this quagmire and get down on themselves for not accomplishing the monetary milestones they need for his or her circle of relatives and his or her own life.

Recall having a good time small victories along with the manner. For instance, congratulate yourself once you pay off your debt, or praise yourself while you stick with your budget for 3 months strong, or while you correctly pad your emergency fund.

In case you are married, you and your partner need to paintings collectively at the budget so that it feels honest to each of you, and you each have the identical level of dedication toward attaining it. This could cross a protracted manner closer to supporting you prevent cash-related arguments. Under are a few suggestions for married couples who want to create a budget collectively:

Don't forget switching to an envelope budgeting system that makes use of cash for spending regions that require a greater subject.

Use budgeting software with a mobile app so you can input spending in real-time.

Pay off Debt

Debt is a large obstacle for plenty about achieving financial desires. It is why you need to make getting rid of it a concern. Set up a debt elimination plan, that will help you pay it off extra fast. For example, while making minimum payments on all your debt debts, pay any extra cash towards one debt at a time. After paying off one debt account, flows all the money you were paying on the primary debt to the following debt and preserve from there, growing a debt-pay down "snowball effect."

Attempt these recommendations that will help you pay off debt greater quick:

Sell unused or unwanted objects around your private home to find extra cash to feature your debt reimbursement plan.

A 2nd job can assist speed up the procedure and can be essential if you need to make speedy or lasting adjustments to your scenario.

Look for areas in which you can reduce your budget to grow the coins to be had on your debt bills.

Don't Be Afraid to invite for a recommendation

As soon as you have grown your savings and want to begin investing to increase your wealth, speak to a monetary planner that will help you make smart funding selections.

An excellent adviser will proportion the dangers involved in every funding and help you discover merchandise that in shape your comfort stage and investing go back wishes while helping you figure toward your goals as quickly as possible. A monetary planner can also help you along with your price range, that's any other plus.

Investing is an extended-term approach that helps you in building wealth. You can also find monetary assist someplace else, such as:

If your dad and mom or other family participants are good with cash, don't forget asking them for assist, and talking to them approximately what worked for them financially and what they might have done in another way.

Getting debt paid off, cash stored and progress made toward your economic dreams would not have to be a difficult experience. Invest in yourself and your monetary future so that you won't ever want to worry about your finances once more.

Beginner's guide to managing your money

Taking the time to manage your money better can pay off. It let you live on top of your bills and shop £1,000s every 12 months. You could use these more savings to pay off any money owed you may have, put them toward your pension, or spend them on your subsequent car or excursion. Read on for cash control recommendations, which include the way to installation a price range, sticking to it and the way to keep.

How to set up a budget

Step one to taking management of your finance is doing a budget.

It'll take a bit effort, however, it's an extremely good manner to get a short picture of the cash you have coming in and going out.

Putting in a finances approach you're:

Less probably to come to be in debt

Much less possibly to get caught out using surprising prices

Much more likely to have a very good credit rating

Much more likely to be regular for a loan or mortgage

Able to spot regions in which you can make financial savings

In a wonderful role to store up for a vacation, a brand new vehicle, or another treat

What you need

To get began on your finances, you'll want to work out how lots you spend on:

Household payments

Living costs

Monetary products (coverage...)

Own family and buddies (gives...)

Travel (vehicle expenses, public delivery...)

Entertainment (holidays, sport, eating places...)

A tremendous manner to exercise session your finance is with our loose and clean-to-use budget planner.

Snatch as lots records as you may approximately your income and spending (bills, bank statements...) and get began.

You may shop for your information and are available to return to it each time you like.

As a substitute, you may set up a budget by the use of a spreadsheet or write it all down on paper.

There also are a few awesome free budgeting apps available and your financial institution or building society may have a web budgeting tool that takes data directly from your transactions.

Getting your finance back on course

In case you're spending extra than you have got coming in, you need to work out where you may cut lower back.

This may be as smooth as making your lunch at home or canceling a health club you don't use.

You could also preserve a spending diary and preserve a word of everything you buy in a month.

Or, in case you do the maximum of your spending with a financial institution card, look at closing month's bank assertion and exercise session wherein your money is going.

Get everybody worried

Get all people in your own family worried about preserving to a price range.

Sit down together and make a plan that you can all keep on with.

Work out how a lot of spending cash is available and agree between you what you'll ever have.

Greater on should you manage cash jointly or one at a time?

Slicing your household bills and your loan

For many of us, family payments make up a massive chew of our spending.

The good news is that it's smooth to keep masses of pounds off your bills by following our suggestions.

You could additionally save masses and even thousands of kilos through shopping around for a brand new loan, or reviewing the only you have already got.

Why it can pay to check your mortgage regularly.

Be flexible

Lifestyles are unpredictable so attempt to review your budget and your spending if there's a trade, or as a minimum every couple of months.

You would possibly get a pay upward push, this means that you could store extra, or you might discover your household payments increase.

Paying off loans and credit score playing cards

When you have loans or owe money on credit playing cards it commonly makes sense to repay the debt that prices the very best fee of interest first.

Examples include:

Credit score playing cards

Store cards, which typically rate the very best costs of a hobby

Private loans from the bank, which normally charge a decrease fee of interest than credit score or store playing cards

It's far important to ensure you don't spoil the terms of your agreements.

So even in case you're focusing on paying down another debt, you ought to pay at the least the minimum on any credit cards and your monthly required payments on any loan agreements.

In case you've already missed credit score card or mortgage payments or in case you're behind with so-called 'priority debts' such as your:

Rent,

Loan,

Court fines,

Power payments,

Council Tax,

Toddler aid

Take recommendation from an unfastened debt advice charity straight away.

Set a savings aim

Use our savings calculator to see how your financial savings will develop.

A few humans locate it difficult to get prompted about saving, but it's frequently a lot easier in case you set a goal.

Your first step is to have a few emergency savings – cash to fall back on if you have an emergency, along with a boiler breakdown or if you can't work for a while.

Try and get three months' worth of costs in a smooth or on the spot get right of entry to the account.

Don't fear if you can't shop this at once, but maintain it as a target to intention for.

Once you've set apart your emergency fund, possible financial savings dreams to do not forget would possibly consist of:

Shopping for a vehicle without putting off a loan

Taking a holiday while not having to fear about the payments when you get back

Having a few extra money to attract on while you're on maternity or paternity go away

Investing your savings

As your savings begin to develop, you may:

It's a super manner to ensure you'll be capable of live extra without difficulty later in existence.

If you're crushed through your debts

Regularly, the hardest part of paying off your debts is taking the first step.

It's clean to experience crushed in case you recognize you're suffering financially.

It's tempting to bury your head in the sand and ignore your financial institution statements and demands for a charge,

however, it received to make the trouble
any better and will make it worse.

Chapter 4: Reducing Expenses

"Beware of little expenses; a small leak will sink a great ship."

~ Benjamin Franklin

There is so much that most people can do to reduce their expenses without really feeling a financial pinch, but it will take a change in mind set. I've included many tips below. Try as many as you that apply to your situation and make sure to take all your savings and apply them to your debt. Once you have used all that apply to your financial situation, don't stop. Get creative and find other ways to cut your expenses.

If you have a family, make sure you enlist their help in repaying your debt. If they do not know you are making a concerted effort to get out of debt, they may resent your sudden change in spending habits.

One thing I have done is keep track of everything I didn't spend and at the end of the day I would log into the account I was paying down (or my emergency fund account) and pay that amount into the account. Even though it may be just $5 or $10 on any given day, the amount you're paying down adds up over a few weeks.

Cut out the little things. One fancy coffee per day can run you $25 per week or more. That's $1300 per year for something you can make at home for pennies. Other items that often fall into this category are breakfast or lunch out during the week.

Pay cash for day to day purchases. If you limit yourself to a small amount of pocket money each day, you will begin to make wiser choices and prioritize your spending. If, at the end of the day, you have any cash left over, apply it to your debt rather than spend it the next day.

Cut $20 from your grocery budget. Purchase more ingredients and fewer already prepared foods or eat less meat or drink water instead of soda. There are many ways you can cut a few dollars here and there from your grocery budget. If you haven't already, switch to a less expensive grocery store.

Buy used items when you can and put the difference into your debt repayment.

Use your public library. Public libraries are a treasure trove of free entertainment. Books, movies, audiobooks, lecture series, all free! Just don't forget to return anything you borrow in a timely manner.

Buy generic. Try store brand items and if you or your family don't notice a difference keep on buying the less expensive item.

Challenge yourself to a month of spending nothing on entertainment. Find local free entertainment and expand your horizons.

Another great challenge is to see how long you can go without eating out. This challenge requires forethought, but aim for 30 or 45 days. Your health and waistline will improve, as well as your budget.

Turn off your lights! Electric rates are going up, so why pay for something you're not even using?

Use a clothes line. Do your laundry on weekends and hang it out to dry. In the winter, you can use a drying rack to dry laundry.

Investigate automatic debt repayment programs. Student loans offer a reduction in interest rate if you use an automatic repayment plan. You'll benefit in two ways: you will spend less on the interest and you will always make the payment on time.

Eliminate services. If you have someone come in to clean your house or do your landscaping, let them go. Put some time aside each week to do this work yourself.

Reduce your charitable giving. This is just a temporary measure and once you are out of debt, you can return to donating to the charities of your choice.

Buy fewer clothes for yourself and your family. Unless you have children who seem to grow out of their clothes every two months, don't buy new clothes for anyone. Kids who are growing like a weed can get clothes from second hand shops until your debt is paid off.

Reduce grooming expenses. It doesn't have to cost an arm and a leg to look nice. Get your hair cut every seven weeks instead of six, no one will notice. Women can also save by doing their own manicures and waxing.

Give up bad habits. Smoking and drinking can cost a fortune and are not good for your body. Giving up smoking and reducing your alcohol consumption will save you money in two ways - by reducing your spending and keeping you healthier.

Turn your thermostat down in the winter. If you don't have a programmable thermostat, turn your heat down to 60 degrees every night when you go to bed and don't turn it up for the short time you are awake before you go to work in the morning. Wear a sweater, socks and shoes in the house and you will be comfortable at 65 degrees. You'll be amazed at how much you will save by heating your home to 65 for only a few hours at night.

Don't use air conditioning unless you must. In some areas of the country, air conditioning is not a luxury, but even there you don't need to have your home cold. All other areas of the country can reduce air conditioning and save a lot on electric costs. As with heating your home, only cool it when you are at home. Experiment with how warm you can comfortably live, and if necessary, use a fan rather than air conditioning.

Reduce your cable bill. Find as much as you can to watch online and then see what channels you can cut. Feeling bold? Cancel your cable service altogether. You'll have more time to do the things you love, rather than watching TV.

Cancel your land line. Unless you live in an area with horrible cell phone service and cannot get a cell phone repeater, you don't need both a cell phone and a land line.

That should get you started in saving money, but don't stop with these 20 ideas. Keep your eyes open for other areas that you can cut back on, even if only for a short time. Once you are out of debt, you can add some of these items back into your budget, as long as you continue to live within your means.

Chapter 5: How To Start Budgeting?

Whatever your financial goal—whether it is getting a car, paying off your debts, or saving for a vacation—budgeting will make it a reality. If you are going to start a budget, you need to know how to do it, and in this chapter, I will share the most effective you can start.

Step One: Set a Goal

You must know what your goals are. Your goals will guide how the rest of your budget should look and will allow you to track your progress relative to objectives. In the previous chapter, I said budgeting does not require one to have an explicit goal. That is still true. However, it is much simpler to start a new habit with a goal in mind because it gives you drive, motivation, and a sense of purpose. It is easier to remain consistent when you have a goal in mind because then you know what's at stake. It is human nature to be inspired by working towards something, especially when the task is challenging. It is far more difficult to do something challenging with no end goal or for no apparent reason. Imagine someone came to you and told you to keep cranking a handle that belongs to a strange object. You keep cranking, and the more you crank, the more tired and tedious it is becoming. You ask the person why they are making you do this, they tell you, "It is very important. Don't stop. Just keep cranking." But then they walk away, leaving you alone in the room. Chances are you're going to feel a little silly, get annoyed, or just stop cranking. You stop because the task seems pointless. But if they told you each time you crank the object you add $5,000 to your bank account, you will be more motivated, and you will work extra hard.

An extreme example, I know, but it puts my point across. Set a clear goal of what you want. If it is a new computer, which one and how much does it cost? If it is a vacation, where are you going, with who, where are you staying, what will you do, and how much does it cost? And all of these goals should have deadlines. You should not try to save for something indefinitely, or until you get there. That kind of indecisiveness allows room for slacking, postponing, or skipping. If your goals are clear and have a timeline, you can track your progress and understand when you need to be more aggressive or relaxed. It is only after you have done this that you can move to the next step.

Step Two: Monitor

Now you know what you want. It is time to look at how you spend your money. You might think you have a pretty good idea of this, but you might be surprised at how much you do not yet know. To do this, you should record everything you spend your money on; it does not matter how big or small the purchase is. Some people keep receipts, some write down their expenses in a book, and some utilize handy apps.

There are pros and cons to each of these alternatives.

Writing down your expenses in a book can be time-consuming, or you might forget some details. The good thing about it is that it is an active process that is visceral and creates a clear association between your spending and your behavior. It is sure to make you more wary and aware. But because of how hard it can be and how hard it is to keep up, I suggest you track your spending electronically.

Using apps is effective, and it is likely to catch all your spending habits if you use your card. In apps like Mint, PocketGuard, Personal Capital, MoneyPatrol, YNAB, EverDollar, and Dollarbird, you can link all your accounts and cards to be able to track all your spending (Bieber, 2018). This is a great, more passive method that avoids the headaches that come with doing it yourself. But you will still have to check if everything in the app is as it should be. If you withdraw cash, the apps won't track how you spend it, so you will need to record it.

To make things easier, consider using the one card method. This is when you use one card as your debit and credit card. If you cannot reduce to one card, use the fewest cards possible. This means there will be fewer threads to follow, which is simpler to work with. The technology will do the rest.

Another thing you should keep your eye on is irregular expenses. These are expenses that creep up on you, they usually come during certain specific seasons or dates. These are things like birthdays, gift-giving holidays, car inspections and registrations, vacations, and others. Start looking at how you spent your money during those periods. Generally, you will see an increase in your spending in those times because it combines your normal spending with unexpected or irregular expenses. A lot of people get into debt or borrow money because of these events. Think of it like this. If you expect to make $200 each month, and you spend all each month, never going over, it might sound like a good budget plan because you are not getting into debt. But what happens when your car breaks down, and you have to fix it? When you take these types of irregular expenses into account, you put yourself in a much better position to predict your behavior.

It might sound like overkill, but I say use as many of these methods as you find comfortable. You will need a hybrid method if you use cash and electronic payments. You might need a notebook to write what you spent your cash on and tracking systems to track other purchases. When I withdraw cash, I write in my notebook when the cash was withdrawn, how much it was, and proceed to record every purchase I made with it. It will take you some time until you find a method and system that works for you perfectly, so be patient when you start engaging in this process. It is okay to make some mistakes, but with time you will get it right. Don't be afraid to experiment, either.

Step Three: Add up All Your Income

You need to know how much money is coming in. If you have a job, add your salary. If your salary is not fixed, you can add the minimum you expect to make in a given period, typically a month. If you have a side gig, you should look to add that money. If you get an allowance from your family or any other financial support source like child support, add it. If it is money coming in, you need to add it. This is important because once you have arrived at a total figure, you can brainstorm on strategies to meet your financial goals. Here is an example of what that might look like.

You might want to save up for a holiday. You might decide to spend 70% of your income and save 30% for the holiday. Since you know your spending habits very well, you would have spotted wasteful spending, and you will know which sacrifices to make. You could cut things like going out, eating out, or ordering in.

Step Four: Look at Where the Money Goes

You now have a clear idea of how you spend your money and how much money you get. Now you should look at where your money goes each month. These are fixed expenses. Things that, whether you like it or not, you spend money on. I call these the immovables because they mostly remain the same. These are things like rent, utilities, insurance, loans, credit card payments, and other payments. Now that you've done this think about what you would like to save a month to reach your goal.

Then subtract your immovables and your desired savings from your take-home income. The money that is left over is money you can spend on what you desire. It is your spending allowance.

Here is an example:

Fixed Expenses/ Immovables

Accommodation: $700

This is your rent or payment on a house. This includes all expenses associated with it, like taxes.

Debt: $200

These are credit cards, loans, car payments, etc.

Fixed payments: $300

These are things like utilities, health insurance, subscriptions (hopefully important ones)

Savings: $200

This is the amount you want to save, or it can include investments. This can serve short-term or long-term goals.

Total = $1,400

That is the amount that the immovables cost a month.

Spending Allowance

Spending allowance = income - immovables

Example of a spending allowance:

$1,800 - $1,400

Spending allowance = $400

Spending allowance is just money left to spend on anything else. This might be food, clothes, or beer.

Step Five: Embrace Help

You should be open to being helped in certain areas. Making a budget can be hard if you are just learning. If that is the problem you face, you should be open to using apps to guide you through setting a budget.

Chapter 6: Breaking Down Your Savings Options

So now that we have discussed that you should be saving, and you have set up your goals. Let's discuss all of your options when it comes to savings. If you only have one bank account for savings, then it may become confusing to look at your balance and figure out which percent of your savings goes to each goal. Not to mention that a savings account at your bank may not be the best account option for you depending on what it is you're saving for. Or if a savings account really is your best option.

No matter which savings decision you make, it won't mean anything if you don't have a system set up to ensure that you are putting money into it regularly. When you have other bills to pay, and your life gets busy, some people think they'll add to their savings at the end of a paycheck and save whatever they have left over. If you are someone who has that mentality, stop it now.

The first option is to set up an automatic transfer. The same way you can set up your bank account to automatically pay your bills on time, you can set it up to transfer a set amount of money from your checking to your savings as regularly as you'd like.

There are a couple different reasons to support why this option is a great one. Like once you set it up, you don't have to think about it anymore. You can cross it off your list and know it's being handled.

The ability to not have to think about it has a couple benefits of its own. For one, it means you don't have to second guess your savings decision every time you make a deposit which also means you'll stay consistent with the amount you have chosen to save. Secondly, if you have more than one savings account, you can set up transfers for each account, deducting different amounts at different times for different saving goals. And lastly, since you'll have a pre-arranged deduction date, you will learn to adapt to living off less money which will make it easier for your savings to grow.

If you don't think an automatic deduction is right for you, don't fret because I have another solution. If you are employed, you may want to discuss options to have a percentage of your income deducted from your paycheck before it even hits your hot little hands. According to Investopedia.com, it is common for employees to deduct a set percentage of their income to contribute to their retirement account. Or to have their premium for their insurance paid to ensure they never miss a payment. And those are just a couple of the many options that most employees have.

Ok, we have now discussed why you should be saving, and options to help you save and stay on track. Now let's talk about the variety of saving methods you can use that will benefit your goals the most.

Choosing the right savings method is going to be dependent on a few different variables so stay with me. You'll need to consider the amount you want to save, how accessible you need the funds to be and how often you'll want/need to withdraw from the account.

For example; if you are setting up your emergency fund account you probably want to make sure you can access that account when you have, well, an emergency. However, if you are saving for retirement, you probably want to use a method that will allow your money to grow interest over time with fewer options to withdraw to ensure your funds stay in the account and you don't become tempted to dip into it before you retire.

There are three broad options to choose from, each with many sub-options within them. They are savings accounts, certificate of deposits (otherwise known as CDs), and retirement.

This savings method is great for your shorter term goals. They are usually one of the easiest savings account options most people think of immediately because they are easy to open and you usually can get one through the bank you already have your checking account through. This option usually offers the lowest interest rates (usually less than 1%) and have few restrictions for access to the account. They also rarely have a required minimum balance, and if it is associated with brick and mortar banks, you can easily access them online or through your bank's app.

Personally speaking, this is the option I chose first because at the time I was overwhelmed with all of the savings options and requirements that I just wanted something simple to start with that would plant the seed of habit of transferring funds into a savings at all. But I was also worried that the amount I predetermined to save may be too much, and I wanted to ensure I would have access to my funds in case I underestimated my expenses between paychecks.

What ended up happening is I became too reliant on the ability and efficiency of which I could transfer my funds back into my checking account that instead of focusing on living within my new found budget I allowed myself to splurge more than just on occasion and repeatedly found my savings account empty. It wasn't until my bank closed my account due to inactivity that I realized I didn't have the discipline to put money in a savings account and leave it alone to grow. However, just because I didn't have the discipline doesn't mean you don't either. This could be a great way to babystep your way into savings.

What I ended up doing was opening an account through an online bank. I'll admit I was skeptical at first because with today's technology and the horror stories that seem to circulate, it seemed totally plausible that I would think I'm giving my money to a bank when in reality it's some fake business scammer pretending to be a bank and get me to provide all my bank information.

Luckily, I was smart enough to do some research on the bank I was eyeing. I even talked to some close friends and family and learned a few of them already had accounts at the same bank and they loved it.

Online banks can be a great option for a savings account because they will typically offer a higher interest rate for savings accounts. They can do this because they usually only exist online and therefore don't have any overhead costs that standard banks have to account for.

The other benefit I found for this option is they have a limit on how often I can transfer funds to or from my account, and the transfer takes three days to hit my checking account. Because of these small regulations, I was being forced to plan ahead for any expenses that may be out of my new-found budget which also made me do less impulse spending. But I feel secure in knowing that if I should need to dip into my savings, I can do so. Not to mention it doesn't hurt that the longer I leave my account alone, I actually have the opportunity to watch it grow from the higher interest rate I'm getting that my previous savings account didn't offer.

Let's not assume you're like I was and starting this from scratch. Maybe you've already gone this route and now have a bit of a cushion and are looking to explore new options that could make your savings grow faster than a 1.65% interest rate. If that's the case, you may want to check out opening a money market account.

According to Investopedia, money market accounts pay high yielding interest based on the current market rates. They can offer a higher interest rate due to requiring a higher minimum balance while limiting the number of withdrawals the account holder can make over any given time. Due to these restrictions, it makes them less liquid than a checking account.

Some banks like State Farm Bank require a $100 initial deposit, whereas Silvergate Bank requires $1000. Similarly, State Farm Bank requires a monthly direct deposit to avoid the pesky service fee, and although Silvergate doesn't require that you deposit into the account every month, you do need to maintain a minimum balance of $1000 to avoid their $15 a month fee.

Moving on, let's discuss CDs (Certificate of Deposit). CD's are a great option for your medium length goals that you know are going to take you awhile to achieve. CD's have a fixed maturity date, a specified fixed interest rate (typically CDs offer the highest interest rate than any other savings options through a bank) and can be issued for any amount outside of the minimum investment required.

To put it simply, you invest whatever amount you want/need into the CD then you decide how long you want the term length to be (a term length is the amount of time you choose to let your money sit before you withdraw the funds). This can range from a few days, months or years depending on the goal you have in place. Once you set these terms you leave it alone to grow.

Having a CD restricts your access to the funds until the "maturity date" has arrived at which point you can choose to either renew it or withdrawal the account. However, if you try and remove any funds before the maturity date has hit, you may face penalties.

Perks of having a CD is you can generally just forget about it until its maturity date, there are no monthly fees and is generally a very low-risk way to save money. However, because of the penalties of withdrawing early, you want to make sure you're in a position where you can set it up and leave it alone. On the plus side, the longer the term length, the longer you commit to keeping your money in the bank which equals a higher interest rate for your return.

Placing your money in an account like this can be a little nerve wracking especially because you can't predict the future and may not feel completely confident that you won't need access to these funds before the maturity date hits. Thankfully there is something called a CD Ladder that may provide you with a little flexibility and avoid the penalties for withdrawing the account.

How it works is like this, say you have $10,000. Instead of placing the full amount into one CD, you split it up and open five CDs ranging from one to five years each. So now you have $2000 in five different CDs. Once the first year is up, you then gain access to the $2000 you placed in the initial one year CD. If you find you need that money, you can cash out without penalty, and still have your other four CDs growing. If you don't need the money, you can reinvest it into a five year CD. The next year, your previously opened two-year CD will be mature, and again, you can reinvest it for a five-year CD the way you did the year before. If you continue this process every year, then you have a steady five-year CD maturing every year. At which point you will have the flexibility to cash out one CD a year without facing early withdrawal penalties. Pretty amazing plan, right?

Chapter 7: Budgeting Process

Making an interpretation of Strategy into Targets and Budgets

There are four measurements to think about when deciphering elevated level technique, for example, crucial, and objectives, into spending plans.

Targets are fundamentally your objectives, e.g., expanding the sum every client spends at your retail location. At that point, you create at least one methodologies to accomplish your objectives. The organization can build client spending through extending item contributions, sourcing new providers, advancement, and so forth.

You have to follow and assess the adequacy of the systems, utilizing significant measures. For instance, you can quantify the normal week by week spending per client and normal value changes as sources of info.

At long last, you should set focuses on that you might want to reach before the finish of a specific period. The objectives ought to be quantifiable and time sensitive, for example, an expansion in the volume of offers or an expansion in the quantity of items sold.

Planning Strategies

Objectives of the Budgeting Process

Planning is a basic procedure for any organizations in a few different ways.

1. Helps in the arranging of genuine activities

The procedure gets directors to think about how conditions may change and what steps they have to take, while additionally enabling supervisors to see how to address issues when they emerge.

2. Co-ordinates the exercises of the association

Planning urges supervisors to assemble associations with different pieces of the activity and see how the different offices and groups connect with one another and how they all help the general association.

3. Imparting plans to different supervisors

Imparting plans to directors is a significant social part of the procedure, which guarantees that everybody gets an unmistakable comprehension of how they bolster the association. It energizes correspondence of individual objectives, plans, and activities, which all move up together to help the development of the business. It additionally guarantees suitable people are made responsible for actualizing the financial limit.

4. Rouses chiefs to endeavor to accomplish the spending objectives

Planning gets administrators to concentrate on interest in the spending procedure. It gives a test or focus to people and chiefs by connecting their pay and execution comparative with the financial limit.

5. Control exercises

Supervisors can contrast genuine going through with the spending limit with control money related **exercises.**

6. Assess the presentation of administrators

Planning gives a methods for advising chiefs regarding how well they are acting in meeting targets they have set.

Sorts of Budgets

A strong spending system is worked around an ace spending plan comprising of working spending plans, capital use spending plans, and money spending plans. The consolidated spending plans produce a planned pay articulation, accounting report, and income proclamation.

1. Working spending plan

Incomes and related costs in everyday activities are planned in detail and are separated into significant classifications, for example, incomes, compensations, benefits, and non-pay costs.

2. Capital spending plan

Capital spending plans are ordinarily demands for acquisition of enormous resources, for example, property, gear, or IT frameworks that make significant requests on an association's income. The reasons for capital spending plans are to assign reserves, control chances in basic leadership, and set needs.

3. Money spending plan

Money spending plans tie the other two spending plans together and consider the planning of installments and the planning of receipt of money from incomes. Money spending plans assist the executives with following and deal with the organization's income successfully by surveying whether extra capital is required, regardless of whether the organization needs to fund-raise, or if there is abundance capital.

Spending Types

Planning Process

The planning procedure for most huge organizations as a rule starts four to a half year before the beginning of the money related year, while some may take a whole monetary year to finish. Most associations set spending plans and embrace fluctuation examination on a month to month premise. Beginning from the underlying arranging stage, the organization experiences a progression of stages to at long last execute the spending limit. Regular procedures incorporate correspondence inside official administration, building up goals and targets, building up a nitty gritty spending plan, aggregation and correction of spending model, spending board of trustees survey, and endorsement.

10 Steps to Developing and Managing a Budget

Each association needs a spending limit. Creating and dealing with a financial limit is the means by which effective organizations apportion, track and plan monetary spending.

A formal planning process is the establishment for good business the board, development and improvement.

Fundamentally the same as our own accounts, order and arranging ought to be the foundation of a business planning process.

So where do we start? Similarly as with most things that accompany dealing with an association, planning should be driven by the vision (what we are attempting to achieve) and the vital arrangement (the means to arrive).

Associations that stay concentrated on their system and plan know precisely where they need to spend their assets and have an arrangement to help prevent them from going through cash in zones that don't agree with the vision (what we are attempting to do) and crucial (we are doing it).

10 Steps to Developing and Managing a Budget

1. Vital Plan

Each association, regardless of the size should know why it exists and what it wants to achieve.

This is verbalized through a composed Vision and Mission Statement. A Strategic Plan is the HOW the association intends to accomplish its crucial.

The initial phase in the planning procedure is having a composed key arrangement. This guarantees authoritative assets are utilized to help the technique and improvement of the association. It implies planning toward the vision.

2. Business Goals

Yearly business objectives are the means an association takes to execute its vital arrangement and it is these objectives that should be supported by the spending limit.

Objectives should be created and there should be responsibility for accomplishing objectives. This is regularly the obligation of the supervisory crew, board or entrepreneur.

The monetary allowance gives the money related assets to accomplish objectives.

For instance, if your association has outgrown its office and there is a target to build space, there should be dollars planned to extend or move the business tasks.

3. Income Projections

Income projections ought to be founded on verifiable money related execution, just as anticipated development salary. The anticipated development might be attached to authoritative objectives and arranged activities that will start business development.

For instance, if there is an objective to expand deals by 10%, those business projections ought to be a piece of the income projections for the year.

4. Fixed Cost Projections

Anticipating fixed expenses is only a question of taking a gander at the month to month unsurprising costs that don't change. Worker remuneration costs, office costs, utility costs, home loan or lease installments, protection costs, and so forth.

Fixed expenses don't change and are a base cost that should be subsidized in the spending limit. For instance, if there are open staff positions, the expense to fill those positions ought to be a piece of fixed cost projections.

5. Variable Cost Projections

Having a formal and organized planning process is the establishment for good business the board, development and development.Variable expenses are costs that vary from month to month, supply costs, extra time costs, and so forth.

These are costs that can and ought to be planned and controlled.

For instance, if higher Christmas deals drive additional time costs briefly, those expenses ought to be planned.

6. Yearly Goal Expenses

Objective related undertakings ought to likewise be given spending plans.

Every activity ought to have anticipated expenses related with the objectives.

This is the place the expense of executing objectives are fused into the yearly spending plan.

Projections of expenses ought to be recognized, spread out and fused into the departmental spending that is answerable for finishing the objective.

For instance, if the business office has an objective of expanding deals by 10%, costs related with the expanded deals (extra advertising materials, travel, stimulation) ought to be joined into that spending limit.

7. Target Profit Margin

Each association, regardless of whether they are for-benefit or not-for-benefit, ought to have a focused on net revenue. Overall revenues take into consideration returns for the entrepreneur or speculators.

Not-revenue driven associations utilize their overall revenues to reinvest into the offices and improvement of the association. Benefits are significant for all associations and sound net revenues are a solid marker of the quality of an association.

8. Board Approval

The administering board, president, proprietor or leader of the association ought to affirm the financial limit and keep current with spending execution. Once more, like your own funds, the proprietor ought to audit month to month fiscal reports for the accompanying reasons.

To screen spending execution.

To be comfortable with all consumptions.

To defend the association against misappropriation of assets or worker misrepresentation.

9. Spending Review

A spending survey board should meet on a month to month premise to screen execution against objectives. This board of trustees should audit spending differences and survey issues related with spending overages.

It is imperative to do this on a month to month premise so there can be a rectification to overspending or change to the financial limit if necessary.

Holding up until the year's end to make revisions could have a negative effect on the last spending result.

10. Managing Budget Variances

Spending changes ought to be audited with the dependable office administrator and questions ought to be raised about what caused the fluctuation.

Now and then unanticipated circumstances emerge that can't be maintained a strategic distance from so it is additionally significant (simply like your own spending limit) to have a secret stash to help with those spontaneous consumptions.

For instance, if the HVAC framework all of a sudden goes down, and should be supplanted, this would be a spending fluctuation that should be subsidized.

Great planning procedures can help create and advance an association, while messy planning and observing of spending plans can bushwhack an association and influence its long haul budgetary wellbeing and suitability.

The spending procedure is an interminable circle like the bigger money related arranging process. It includes characterizing objectives and social event information;

framing desires and accommodating objectives and information;

making the spending limit;

observing genuine results and examining fluctuations;

altering spending plan, desires, or objectives;

reclassifying objectives.

Chapter 8: Live Within Your Means

If you find yourself spending more than you are saving and gradually going into debt, you need to discipline yourself and create an action plan. Learn how to create a budget and live within your means. Have sufficient savings, emergency funds, and less credit card debt. If you have difficulty trying to live within your means, follow these tips to help you get back on the right track:

Identify your wants and needs and know the difference between the two. What are the things that you want to have? What are the things that you actually need and cannot live without? The things that you want may be luxurious items, such as jewelry, an expensive smartphone, or a new car. If you think about it deeply, you don't really need these things to survive. You can get by without wearing jewelry. You can use a less expensive phone to communicate with other people. You can buy a less expensive car model or simply use public transportation.

The things you need, however, are necessities and are absolutely important. These things include food, shelter, clothing, water and electricity. Obviously, you need to pay your water and electric bills, as well as buy food. Then again, even though clothing is necessary, you should avoid buying branded clothes that you don't really need. Check out your closet and see if your clothes can still be worn, so you will not be tempted to buy new ones on impulse.

Set guidelines.

Everyone has a different budget depending on their wants and needs. Nevertheless, if ever you need to make adjustments, see to it that you make up for the amounts that you subtract. For instance, you may suddenly have to fly to another state to visit family or purchase something that you did not plan to purchase initially. In these cases, you have to make adjustments with your budget to make sure that you stay within your spending limit and do not go overboard. Track and trim your expenses. Keep track of your expenses so you know exactly where your money goes. At the end of each week or month, find out which areas you can cut back on. For instance, you can cut back on your electric bill by turning off the air conditioning unit after a few hours, instead of leaving it on overnight. You may also replace your refrigerator for a smaller unit if possible. Instead of turning on the water sprinklers, use recycled water to water the plants and flowers in your garden. Doing so can help you cut back on your water bill. Use the SMART method. Have you ever heard of the SMART method? It stands for Specific, Measurable, Attainable, Relevant and Time-Related. Your goals should be specific, so you can determine the action that you need to take. For instance, instead of saying that you have to 'save money', you should be clearer and say that you have to 'save enough money to go on a vacation abroad'. Your goal should also be measurable and you should know how close you are to it. For instance, if you need $2,000 for your vacation abroad, you are near if you've already saved $1,300. You also have to set goals that are attainable and realistic. It may take a few months before you reach $2,000, but it's possible if you save enough money per week.

Your goal has to be relevant, too. It has to fit your needs. For instance, you may want to stay in a nice hotel when you get to your destination. Finally, it has to be time-related. You must set a specific target date. When do you want to go on a vacation abroad? Do you want to go there in the summer, in Christmas, or on your birthday week? You have to be clear.

Chapter 9: Looking For Solutions That Work

The solutions for the budgeting challenges vary depending on the difficulties that you are facing. In this chapter, we will suggest ways on how you can make your budget fit until the next payday. The budget, in this case, is the amount of money left after you set aside your savings.

Identifying your primary expenses

After you put your savings in a separate account, the next step is to pay for all the necessary expenses and your past financial commitments. The biggest chunk of your money will go to your food, rent and utilities expenses.

Food

You want to minimize your food expenses to make sure that your budget will fit until the next pay day. Ideally, you should make your own food to ensure that you get the most nutrition from the amount that you spend. If you are fond of eating out, you may need to stop this habit. For the price of a meal in a restaurant, you will be able to make at least three times the amount of food if you prepare it yourself. Of course, you also need to consider the amount of time that you will spend preparing your food. However, home cooked food is generally healthier than the alternatives.

Rent

Next to the food expenses, you will also need to pay for your lodging cost. The rule for saving on your lodging expenses is to live in a place that will fit your budget.

The amount that you need will vary based on your location. If the rent is eating up too much of the budget, you should consider allocating some of your savings for your food and other expenses to pay for your rent.

In some cases, you may also need to consider moving to a new home. By moving to a better location, you may be able to lessen your rent expenses. In some cases, you may also lessen your average transportation cost. This could happen if you move to a place that is closer to your usual destinations like the office or the school of your child. The best strategy to use here will vary, depending on the situation you are in.

Utility bills

You may also lessen your expenses through your utility bills. If you do not manage this type of spending properly, you may also end up going over your budget. Ideally, you want to make sure that you only sign up for the services that you need.

For instance, if no one is watching TV in your home, there is probably no need to have a TV service connected. The same goes with your home internet connection and your mobile phone subscription. You should only apply for the right amount of internet capping that you need, based on your usage history.

With your mobile phone for example, if you mostly use Wi-Fi from your home internet and from your work, you may want to choose a plan with limited data subscription. Data usage fees are the most common types of accidental spending in mobile phone bills. If data usage is a problem for you or any of your family members, you might as well have the service removed, and rely solely on Wi-Fi for your internet usage.

Lastly, you need to find solutions for the accidental expenses that may come out of your utility bills. It is common for utility service companies to charge you automatically without warning. If you made a long distance call, for instance, without realizing it, you will only know about it in your next phone bill.

If you experience getting an inflated bill in any of the services you use, make sure to contact the companies that provide the service. Ask them why your bill is bigger than usual. If the issue cannot be resolved and you cannot get any deductions on your bill, the next best thing is to try to have the issue resolved so that the extra expenses do not happen again. If you are getting accidental long distance calls on your mobile phone, you may ask for an add-on that will block all long distance phone calls. You could then have all your long distance calls using online methods.

If your water bill is inflated, there may be a leak somewhere in your home. You will need to find this leak and have it sealed. In some cases, the only possible solution to an inflated service bill is to modify your usage behavior. If you keep going over your mobile phone call minutes, for example, you may need to adjust your calling behavior or use alternative services to contact the people important to you.

For your electricity usage, on the other hand, there are times when the bill just spikes up. In the summer months, for instance, we tend to crank the air conditioning up to make the interior of the home colder. In contrast, we turn up the heat during the cold winter months. These services will affect your bills and your budget. You will need to prepare your budget by allocating a bigger amount for the essential services for these special months.

Lifestyle expenses

Life would be boring if you only spend on the most important things. Every now and then, you may feel the need to dine out or to buy something that makes you feel good. You can still enjoy these types of spending. However you will need to put a cap on the amount you spend by setting a lifestyle budget.

To define this allocation, you may use it for any purchase or experience that makes you happy. Ideally, you should use it to give yourself rewards for working hard. You do not need to spend all the money you set aside for your lifestyle expenses. Instead, you can also save it to create a fund that you can use for enjoyable experiences. For example, you can save for a travel vacation. You could also use the fund for a shopping spree on your birthday. The choice is all yours on how you will use this fund.

Ideally, this fund should not take up more than 10% of your income. However, you may adjust this amount, depending on your preferences.

Cut back in some areas of your lifestyle

When creating this plan, you will find that you are spending too much on some areas of your life. Some of us, for example, are spending too much in our lifestyle expenses. If this is the case, there may be a need to cut back on buying unnecessary things and paying for unnecessary experiences.

In some cases, some of our bills may balloon out of proportion. In this case, you may need to adjust your behavior or have safeguards put in place to prevent this from happening again in the future.

Create new habits on how you use your money

Many of our bad spending habits can be removed just by creating new habits. One of the first habits that you need to adopt is to set aside most the money that will be allocated to your savings first. You can do this by transferring the money from your payroll account straight to your savings account right after your receive it. You can have both accounts set up in the same bank so that you do not have to travel to do this task. Ideally, your savings account should not have an ATM card so that you can only take money out from it if you really plan it.

After setting aside your savings, the next habit to create is allocating the money for food, your bills and your rent. Next to your savings, these expenses are the most important because they are needed to keep you a functioning member of society.

By ensuring that you have the funds to pay for these expenses, you will be able to have peace of mind until you get your next paycheck.

Lastly, you should set aside the amount you need for your emergency fund and your lifestyle fund. These two are less important than the other expenses because they are not as urgent. At this point, you will often find that there is only a small amount left for you to spend freely.

By developing these habits, you will be able to limit the spending rush that comes after every payday. It is common for people to think and feel like they are wealthy right after receiving their pay. It is also common for people to go out and have drinks or to go on a shopping spree when they have this feeling. By implementing the habits discussed above, you will not have the same feeling and you will be able to prevent your spending sprees.

Anticipating irresistible spending and preparing for them

There are times when we will fail in stopping our old habits. After getting a paycheck, for instance, you may pass by a shop you used to go to in the past and spend more than your allocated lifestyle amount.

This is common for people whose past habits still have a strong influence on their behavior. The triggers of your old habits may lead you to relapse. The best way to prevent this is by anticipating the old habits and their effects on your mind.

People who used to splurge on buffets for example, may be tempted to spend too much if they see and smell the food in a buffet restaurant. If they can anticipate this, it is possible to eat before going to places with buffets so that they will not overspend.

You can also do the same for your old habits. If there is a habit that you are trying to avoid for your budgeting to work, you will need to anticipate and make preparations for it. If you cannot prevent them from happening, you can avoid the habit altogether by avoiding going to certain places.

Building up the necessary funds

It may also be important for you to allocate some money to your emergency funds. If you put a small amount of money aside, you will have a fund that can be solely used for emergencies of any nature. This is commonly used for medical emergencies. However, the fund can also be used in many other ways.

For instance, this fund can be used for when you are transitioning from one job to another. When you lose your job for example, you will no longer have income to support your lifestyle. It is common for people to use their savings fund when this happens. If this happens, you will lose whatever momentum you have in saving for your goal.

Your emergency fund will serve as your lifeline while you look for a new job. You will use this fund for your daily needs so that you do not touch your savings. The rule of thumb is to have your emergency fund equal to six times your monthly expenses. If you spend a total of $1,000 on average per month, you should have an emergency fund of at least $6,000. This way, you will have a six-month window to find a new job without using any part of your goal fund.

It is also important to remember to replenish your emergency fund every time you use a part of it. This will ensure that you will still have a fund to rely on, in case of another emergency.

You do not have to save for your emergency fund all at once. If the amount is too big for you, do not be intimidated by it. Instead, think of an amount that you can comfortably save from your monthly income. Add this amount to your emergency fund every month.

For example, you could choose to only save $100 or $200 from your monthly income. This way, you will eventually reach your target emergency fund amount after 60 months. Because emergencies are few and far between, you may not need your emergency fund while saving for it.

After reaching your target amount, you should just stop adding more to your emergency fund. It is important though to keep the fund in a savings account so that you will be able to access it in case of a true emergency.

It may also be necessary for you to define what constitutes an emergency so that you will not spend the fund on anything unimportant. This is especially necessary if more than one person has access to the fund. For example, you can say that the emergency fund should only be used for medical emergencies, for urgent fixes around the house, for exceptionally high utility bills and the likes. By defining what purpose the emergency fund is for, the people who have access to it will not use it for unnecessary spending.

Write down the changes that need to be made

After identifying all the necessary expenses and the changes that need to be made, you need to write them down on paper. In particular, you want to take note of all the non-negotiable expenses. This includes the expenses discussed above like food, rent, and all your bills. You may also need to list down all the things that you need to do to cut back in some of these areas.

If you have additional ideas on how you or the members of your household can limit your expenses, you should also include them here. This list will be a handy reference when you implement your plans later on.

Chapter 10: Recording Your Income

The second kind of financial data that you need to be familiar with is your income. Basically, it is the opposite of your expenses. If your expenses refer to the money that you spend, your income refers to the money that you make.

Typically, if you are an employee, your income is fixed. Every month, you receive a specific amount of money sans incentives and bonuses. However, if you are an entrepreneur, your income is variable. It will depend on the amount of sales that you have made for the month. However, it can also be a mix of both. There are some employees who engage themselves in small businesses to produce a little income on the side. Accounts receivable also fall under this category. Your accounts receivable refer to the money that you are expecting to receive. An example of this is when you have lent someone a certain amount of cash. The money that he pays you back is recorded under this category. Whatever your source of income is, it is important you determine how much you make in a month.

Take out the pay slips or business records that you gathered so that you can start recording your income data. In your record book, a few spaces below your expenses, create a space for your income. To avoid confusing it with your previously encoded data, write "INCOME." List the sources of your income, including how much money you have received from each. Add up each amount and write down the total. Your list should look like this:

INCOME FOR THE MONTH OF _____

1. Monthly salary	$5,000
2. Incentives and bonuses	$450
3. Income from small business	$500

TOTAL INCOME   **$5,950**

If you are making a budget for your home and let's say, for example, both you and your husband are working to sustain the needs of your family, your list can look like this:

INCOME FOR THE MONTH OF _____

1. Monthly salary (dad) $5,000

2. Monthly salary (mom) $4,500

3. Incentives and bonuses $300 (dad)

4. Incentives and bonuses $500 (mom)

TOTAL INCOME   **$10,300**

Your list may vary according to your circumstances. Just be sure to list and total all your income data and double check your records. Compare it with the financial documents that you have on hand and redo your calculations just to be safe.

Chapter 11: Budget Busts 1 And 2 - College And Housing

We've gone through how to create a pretty basic budget, but there are certain things in a person's life that really affect how they budget. The biggest four are arguably college, housing, debt, and retirement. This chapter will cover the first two: college and housing. For college, that means both saving for your kid's college as a parent and also paying off loans as a recent graduate. Housing is also a huge part of a budget, because everyone needs to live somewhere, whether they're renting or buying. We'll go over both potential budget busts thoroughly in this chapter.

Paying for college (before and after)

When you become a parent, your budget changes dramatically. You are now financially responsible for another human being for the next 18 years or so. For many parents, that means saving up for their kids' college. How much do you need to put away each month? It depends on how much tuition you plan on covering. There are calculators online that can project how much you need based on how many years are left before the kid heads off and how expensive their college might be.

You also need to think about what kind of savings account you're putting the money in. There are plans and accounts specific to building up compound interest, like an Education Savings Account or 529 account, so do research before squirreling away your money. The Savings For College website has a calculator based on the 529 plan, where you enter relevant info like your income, how old your kid is, and so on.

What if the student is on their own financially?

Why have we been addressing just the parents? It's pretty much impossible for a kid to pay their own way through college.

Even if they start working as soon as they legally can, they most likely won't be able to make enough money to pay for more than just a few classes, even at the most affordable community college. If a student is not going to be receiving help from their parents, they do still have some options. No matter what the arrangement is between parents and a student, the adult **needs** to file the FAFSA. The government doesn't care if parents are going to help financially, they only want to know what the parents can technically contribute. If the parents don't file, the kid won't get any help from the feds. A student should also apply for as many scholarships as they qualify for using a database like Fastweb. There are tons of resources out there for both students and parents about paying for college, which that we won't get into now, but just know that the information is out there.

Paying back student loans

Most people leave college with at least some student debt. The average is

$25,000. Interest on student loans tends to be high, around 6.8% (or even higher), and they use a 10-year repayment plan. That translates to almost $300 a month. That number might be different depending on the repayment plan, but the bottom line is, most college graduates end up paying student loans for years and years. This means anyone with student debt should have a budget. If you don't, you could end up in really big trouble, with ballooning loan interest following you much longer than you anticipated. Here are some tips on how to live life with student debt:

#1: Put off big purchases for at least 1-2 years after college.

This includes moving out on your own, getting a pet, getting a car, and so on. You might be excited to get out there and live like a real "adult," but the poor college student lifestyle has a lot of benefits. You'll be able to take out a nice chunk of your student loans if you keep up the starving-student act, but are making more money at a new job. Pour as much of that new salary into your loans as possible.

#2: Find a side job

If you want extra pocket change to offset what you're paying in loans, or you want more money to go towards your loans, you'll have to generate more income. A side job of some kind is a great idea, especially if you have the time. Consider dog-walking, pet-sitting, babysitting, cutting hair, copywriting, tutoring, or employing some other talent you have. In general, the more time and effort you put in your side hustle, the more money it will generate. Figure out how much money you want to make, and then you'll be get a clearer idea of how much work it will be.

#3: Pay more than the required minimum on your loan

The minimum payment is what you are legally obligated to pay, but you are more than free to pay more. If you can, this is a great strategy, because it ensures you don't build up interest, and it lets you pay off the loan faster. Whenever you get a bigger influx of cash for some reason (Christmas bonus, successful side hustle project, etc), devote most, if not all of it, to your loans. Spending it on yourself will be a temptation, but keep the big picture in mind. The sooner that loan is paid, the sooner all that money is back in your pocket.

#4: Make more than one payment per month

In the same vein of paying more than the minimum, paying more than once each month speeds up the process. Consider budgeting for a payment each time you get a paycheck or paying at the beginning of the month and at the end. Make sure the amount you pay is more than the minimum. This is basically the same strategy as tip #3, but dividing up extra payments may be better for some people based on when they get their income.

What to do if you're behind student loan repayments

No one wants to be in a position where they are behind payments on their student loans, but it can happen. What do you do next? The first thing you need to do is contact your lender. They won't stop calling or emailing you just because you're ignoring them. After that's done, there are three possible steps you can take:

#1: Change your repayment plan

Unable to pay the minimum amount? You may be able to change your plan, so you owe less per month. Income-based repayment options are determined based on how much money you're making, so it's about percentages. This will probably extend your loan so you're paying for the next 20 years as opposed to 10, and you'll end up paying more overall, but it's the best option all around if you find yourself behind on payments and unable to pay them.

#2: Find out if you're eligible for loan forgiveness

If you're in a certain field, you might be eligible for loan forgiveness. This won't cancel out your loan entirely, but it can reduce how much you owe, so you don't have pay as much every month. If you are in public service, a teacher, or a healthcare worker, you might qualify for a loan forgiveness program.

#3. Suspend your loan payments

If you cannot pay your loans because of a major life event like job loss, you may be able to suspend them for 3-5 years. Remember that the interest will continue to grow, however, so you will end up owing more than you do now. However, you will also be in a better financial situation once this crisis has passed. The other option in a situation where you currently **cannot** make any payments would be to default, which is very much a last resort, and it has serious consequences.

Budgeting for housing

A budget will be affected by the type of housing you're currently occupying and your future housing goals. Renting an apartment and want to buy a house? Your budget will be a bit different than someone paying a mortgage on a condo they've lived in for 10 years. Let's say you want to move and you want to know what you can afford. According to legendary financial guru Dave Ramsey, your housing costs (no matter what kind of housing) should not cost more than 25% of the income you take home. If your current housing costs more than that, it can be a problem. Saving and paying off debt may be tricky. Here's what to do and budgeting factors to consider when you want to move:

Understand the market

How much do houses or apartments cost around you? Depending on where you live, there can be a huge difference. Talk to a real estate agent, research listings, and so on to get a clearer idea of what you can get with 25% (or less) of your income. It can be tempting to look at housing that would cost more than 25%, because it gets you everything you want, but long-term, going over that limit can be negative consequences. Even if you anticipate making more money in the future, nothing in life is guaranteed, and you don't want to end up stuck in a place you can't afford without sacrificing other goals or things you want.

Anticipate additional costs

There are other fees associated with home ownership and even renting. For renters, you pay for stuff like renter's insurance, security deposit, and more. Be sure to look at utilities and see what's covered in the rent, and what you're responsible for. For home ownership, there are also additional expenses like possible renovations, insurance, **all** utilities, property taxes, etc. There will also be more ongoing expenses like home repairs, which you may not have paid with your previous housing, if you were a renter. These additional costs really add up, and should be factored into the 25% housing cost limit.

Think about other future financial goals

When figuring out your housing budget, calculations don't stop with your current expenses. What else are you saving up for? A new car? Maybe you want to start a family soon, and kids aren't free. You may want to increase your savings for these other financial goals, which means your housing budget shrinks a little. This reflects your **true** housing budget, so don't forget this step.

Tweak your budget based on the information you just got

You have your budget for housing. Are you okay with it? Or do you want to save more? Maybe you have some debt you want to pay off first, so you can use the money that's going towards those payments for housing. It's time to tweak your budget and reduce expenses in other areas. We'll get into debt in the next chapter before giving you tips on reducing expenses in Chapter 6.

Chapter 12: Budgeting Your Money Takes Discipline

Budgeting your finances can be rather difficult and frustrating at times, especially if you have a weakness with compulsive purchases - such as shopping for those new and exciting hot items you desire. Realizing you need to set up a budget because you are spending too much is one of the first steps in making a financial change for the better. Many individuals do not come to the realization that they need to set up a budget until they are so deep in debt and are hurting financially to stay afloat. Don't worry, if this describes you, I have been there and I have pulled myself out. Do not let this situation catch you off guard; act now and recognize that you need to be budgeting your finances in order to become financially fit.

After you have realized that you need a budget, one of the first and most difficult steps of budgeting is setting it up. By creating a budget and successfully implementing it, you will be able to see some options you have with your money, such as growing your money (investing), savings and identifying cost cutting opportunities within the budget you want to create. Also, from carrying out a successful budget, you will be able to recognize that you are a happier person because much financial stress has been lifted by tracking your money. Most of all, you will be creating new financial discipline that will last your entire life.

When setting up your budget, you need to gather and write down all of your expenses. Write down every monthly bill that you have (i.e., rent, mortgage, car payment, insurance, utilities, etc.), and how much you spend on all of the other areas in your life (i.e., groceries, eating out, and activities). You should also write down how much you save each month in a savings account and for retirement, so you can include them in your budget as expenses.

When you have a list of bills, their amounts, and when they are due - you need to decide how much you will need to set aside for each bill from your income each time you get paid. A little secret that I use is to divide up the amounts of your larger bills based on how many times you get paid each month - for example, let's say your rent was $800 per month, and you get paid twice a month; you would set aside $400 from each paycheck, so you don't get hit by $800 in one paycheck. When you implement this strategy, you will notice that you have more money left over on the paycheck when your rent is due.

The ultimate goal for your budget is to stay just below budget, meaning not to spend more than you bring home (your income). Budgeting and spending money is a task of self-control every day. You will need to have the desire, dedication, determination, and most of all the discipline to become an expert at budgeting your money. Remember, if you are not controlling your money, it is more than likely controlling you and you are only harming your financial future.

There are many ways to track your budgeted finances - for example; you can use spreadsheets on your computer (excel), money programs such as Quicken, plain paper to write down everything, transaction records and apps on a tablet or smart phone. There is no right or wrong way to track your finances as long as it works for you and your situation. However, from my experience and millions of others, the budgeting software available today can save you countless hours of your time in helping you track your finances. Many of the software programs can sync with all of your bank accounts, retirement accounts, mortgages, loans, and credit cards to help track your finances. With some of the programs you are even able to enter your budgeted amounts to help you stay on track of being just below budget.

With the tools available today, some basic guiding principles, and your determination and discipline, you too can have a successful budget that can lead to a more financially free life.

Chapter 13: Setting Financial Goals

The first two chapters in this book were written for two purposes: to make you aware of what you need when it comes to managing money and to let you get a realistic view of your current financial situation. After getting an impression of how much money you can potentially apply to your loans without having to sacrifice your lifestyle or having to open another loan account, it is time that you cement your strategy in the form of goals. This chapter now teaches you how to do that.

When it comes to goal-setting, you can never run away from this acronym: SMARTER. This acronym summarizes what goals should be like: specific, measurable, attainable, realistic, evaluate and re-evaluate. The last two components are essential because as you progress through life, you'll make decisions that will affect your goals. For this reason, you need to be flexible to accommodate changes.

Setting specific goals

For you to make a goal specific, you can divide it into three general categories: short-term, medium-term, and long-term. Both the short-term and the medium-term goals are goals in themselves only that they are instrumental in nature. This means that they are stepping stones towards the attainment of your long-term goal. Here's an example of goal statements:

Short-term goal: to save money each month

Medium-term goal: to save money in one year

Long-term goal: to pay off my auto loan

Making goals measurable

For goals to be measurable, you need to have a baseline. This baseline determines whether or not you are successful in attaining that goal within the timeline provided. To make the three goals above measurable, you can modify them this way:

Short-term goal: to save $400 each month

Medium-term goal: to save $4800 in by the end of the year

Long-term goal: to pay off my auto loan balance within three years

Making goals attainable

Goals are attainable only if you have a specific plan of action in order to attain them. If we take the three goals stated above as an example, the short-term and the medium-term goals are the plans of action that makes the long-term goal attainable. Hence, you can still modify the goal statements as follows:

Short-term goal: to save $400 each month by scheduling an automatic transfer from my payroll account to my savings account

Medium-term goal: to save $4800 within the next 12 months by not making withdrawals from my savings account

Long-term goal: to pay off my auto loan account within three years by continuously depositing money into my savings account

Making goals realistic

The realistic element in financial goals deals with practicality. This factor is dependent on the attainable aspect of the goal. It can be said that if a goal is not attainable, then it is not realistic enough. How then can we make the goal statements realistic? It's by considering the time and the other factors that might affect our commitment. For example, if we're looking towards switching jobs, then we might not continuously save money until we get employed. Therefore, if we do not anticipate any challenges in pursuit of our goal, the goals statements will stay the same:

Short-term goal: to save $400 each month by scheduling an automatic transfer from my payroll account to my savings account

Medium-term goal: to save $4800 within the next 12 months by not making withdrawals from my savings account

Long-term goal: to pay off my auto loan account within three years by continuously depositing money into my savings account

Making goals time-bound

Because we already have included a time element in our goal statements ($400 each month, $4800 in 12 months, and loan repayment in three years), we can finally make our goals time-bound by identifying the time when we want to start working. Our goals will then become:

Short-term goal: to save $400 each month by scheduling an automatic transfer from my payroll account to my savings account starting next month

Medium-term goal: to save $4800 within the next 12 months by not making withdrawals from my savings account starting next month

Long-term goal: to pay off my auto loan account within three years by continuously depositing money into my savings account starting next month

Evaluating and re-evaluating your financial goals

Now that we have written three goals statements following SMART, it is time that we think about the possible challenges we'll meet along the way, and how we can use these challenges to evaluate the merits of our goals. In this regard, a high level of flexibility is required not only on our goals but for us as well.

For example, in view of the goals statements we're working on, what might we do in case we encounter an emergency and have to make a withdrawal from our savings account? If the interest rate on the auto loan changes, what sort of changes will we make on the amount we're trying to save? What about if we experience a pay cut? What happens to our target savings each month?

There are a lot of things that might happen in a span of three years. For this reason, can we accommodate such changes and make changes to our goal even if it means changing the three-year to a four-year plan? And what happens if we finally pay off all of our debts?

Chapter 14: The Key To Successful Budgeting

The first rule to follow when creating a budget is to stick to it. Actually, that may be the only rule. Going over the budget can happen easily when you lose sight of your financial goals. Instead of remembering these goals, you focus on the present gratification and forget the reasons for having a budget in the first place. It happens, it's true. Those who want to attain their financial goals must strive to stick to their budget. For example, many newly married couples are saving up for a new house and both may agree to limit their shopping expenses. However, one or both of them might overspend when they lose sight of their long-term goal. It helps always to keep your financial goals in mind so that you can avoid overspending and keep your budget.

It also helps to keep a journal. A financially successful man revealed that he carried around with him an expense journal where he jotted down every expense he made. At the end of the day, he would study the notebook and he would often be surprised to see the things he paid for during that day. He would do the same every day and watch how his expenses decreased as he grew aware of his unnecessary expenditures. Listing down all the things you spend your money on can open your eyes to your expenses. Through this method, you can slowly weed out some of your expenses. Doing that can help your budget and financial goals.

Remember your list of necessities and optional expenses? Never use the money for necessities on your optional expenses. Some people make the mistake of 'borrowing' the money for the electric bill payment, since it won't be due till the end of the month anyway, using the money for something else. However, getting into this habit may not be very useful for your budgeting. It could mess up your financial plans, and you could end up in a house without electricity when you fail to pay your bills on time. This is another part of what sticking to your budget means. You don't move around allotted funds to cover other kinds of expenses. Always bear in mind the difference between priorities and luxuries. You can only spend for luxuries when you've segregated the funds for your basic needs.

Use a rewards system to keep you motivated. Having a budget absolutely does not mean that you have to be unhappy. It doesn't mean that you can't buy nice clothes anymore, or dine out at a restaurant. If you think of it that way, you might end up feeling unhappy about the whole idea. As a result, it can be very easy just to forget about budgeting and spend your money the way you want. To avoid this situation, reward yourself every time you attain a short-term or long-term financial goal. If for this month you were able to cut down on expenses and deposit a small amount in your savings account then congratulate yourself! Buy yourself something that is within your budget, or enjoy a meal with the family in your favorite restaurant. Don't become a slave to your own budget! Remember that you have the power to control your income and expenses.

Chapter 15: The First 10%: The Principle Of Saving

Saving is simply setting aside a portion of your income for future use.

Saving holds the key to financial prosperity but it is not an easy thing for most people. Have you ever noticed that it is when you decide to start saving that some funny urgent financial need crops up to defeat the purpose?

William Feather once said "Just as soon as we make a good resolution, we get into a situation that makes the observance unbearable"

The day you decide to do away with the cakes and cookies and start observing a diet in order to lose weight is the day you begin to get series of invitations to parties and lunch dates that somehow weren't forthcoming before you made that decision.

This is probably the universes' way of testing our commitments to purposes. However, just like any other art, saving can be learnt and mastered.

The first secret of successful saving is to start! The second secret is to be stubborn about it. It might seem hard in the beginning but it gets easier as you continue and now that you know that those 'tests' would come, you should prepare for it and find a way of meeting those expenses without touching your savings.

The First 10%

There's a popular adage that says "A rich man always sets aside one tenth of his coin".

The first 10% of your income should always be put aside as your savings regardless of how much you earn. This 10% would serve as a seed that would be used to generate more wealth for you through investment and wealth acquisition.

So whether you earn a thousand dollars monthly or a million dollars, ensure that you always set aside 10% of it. Even if you earn $100 a month, if you set aside 10% of that every month, by the end of the year, you would have a whopping $100 in your savings account assuming you did not even invest at all.

It might seem like a meager sum in the beginning but as it continues to accumulate and as you invest it, you will realize it isn't (remember the 80/20 rule).

How to Make the Art of Savings Easier

Saving is a habit. It's not always easy to commit to any habit at all and saving is not an exception but with efforts, commitments and consistency, it becomes a part of you such that you begin to enjoy it especially when you start seeing results.

Here are a few tips to help you master the art of savings:

Treat it as Extra Tax: Treat your 10% savings the same way you would treat your taxes. Treat it as money that you own but you cannot access.

Treat it as a Reduction in Income: You can only spend what is available to you or what you have earned hence you should treat your 10% savings money as though there was a sudden cut in your income that you have absolutely no control over.

Always Have a Budget: Lastly, you must always have a budget. A budget serves as a financial blueprint. It guides your spending and helps you avoid frivolous spending.

The Parkinson's Law

When you are preparing your budget, it is important to take note of something known as the Parkinson's Law.

The Parkinson's Law states that all expenses always rise to meet income. If your income improves from $1,000 to $2,000 today, you'll begin to see new things of higher costs to buy; a better car, a better home and so many other things.

So your low income is never an excuse for you not to set aside some part of your income as savings because even if you earned $20,000 monthly, if you don't have strong savings habit and investment knowledge, you will probably die a poor man.

After you've understood the importance of saving, the next bit is growing your savings by not only saving more but investing more to make money to start working for you.

Chapter 16: The Envelope Method

The envelope method is the simplest way to budget. This is the method that has been taught to young people for years before budgeting software and apps were commonplace. All you need are some regular mailing envelopes and somewhere safe to keep them.

Why It Works

The envelope method works well for people who need to visually see what they need to pay and where their money is going. It is also a great way to budget if you aren't good with computers or number crunching. Budgeting using envelopes also works extremely well for people who pay using cash.

If you don't have a checking account or prefer to work with cash then envelope budgeting is extremely helpful. It allows you to set aside money so that it isn't just sitting in your wallet. This way you don't spend money that you need for a particular expense.

The Process

To use the envelope method you will need to have some mailing envelopes and a safe place to store them. A fire safe is fairly inexpensive. You can get a small one for around $50. Not only will having your money stored out of sight help you keep from spending it, it will also help keep it from being stolen.

You will need to first determine your most basic expenses that you need to budget for. Make a list of every type of expense you will have throughout the month. You will then create an envelope for each expense on your list. Here is an example list:

- Rent

- Electric bill

- Gas bill

- Water bill

- Phone bill

- Car payment

- Gasoline

- Groceries

- Household items

- Dining and Entertainment

If you don't have a savings account you may also want to make a list of savings goals. You would then have an envelope for each of those as well. These are usually short term savings goals such as:

- Buying new tires for your car

- Buying a computer, television or other big ticket item

- Buying needed furniture or beds

- Buying needed clothing

- Saving for an anticipated move

- Fund for unexpected car maintenance

- Fun for other unexpected expenses

On each envelope write the name of the expense and the amount you need to put into the envelope each month. For savings envelopes write the total amount you want to save for that item. Number your savings envelopes in order of priority.

When you get money you will divide it into your necessary envelopes. Start with the most important expenses such as rent, utilities and groceries. If you drive your car payment and gasoline will need to come next. Save non-essential expenses for last. Once all of your expense envelopes have the correct amount in them you can begin dividing the rest into your savings envelopes.

It is likely that you get paid more than once per month, but most of your bills will be paid only once per month. It is best if you pay all of your bills at the first of the month. In order to do this you will need to put some money aside each paycheck to each monthly bill. Then at the beginning of the month you will have the money you need to pay each of your bills. Examples of monthly bills are rent and utilities.

Your variable expenses that occur throughout the month on an almost daily basis will be handled a bit differently. After you have put money aside in the monthly bill envelopes you will place money into your variable expense envelopes. Make sure that you have the minimum amount for your pay period in the envelopes. For example, you may have budgeted $400 for groceries for the month. If you get paid weekly you would put $100 per week into the envelope.

As you proceed through the month, use the money in each envelope only for that expense to which it is dedicated. If you really want to go out to eat but your dining envelope is empty, don't take money out of the grocery envelope to satisfy your craving. It is important that you only use the money for what it has been set aside.

Gauging Success

The envelope method doesn't really use precise expense tracking. You don't record each purchase or figure out exactly what you spent the money on. Instead, your success is gauged by what is left in your envelopes and if you have met all of your responsibilities for the month.

If your savings envelopes are gradually increasing then you know you are doing a great job. The more money you are able to save the more clear it is that you are staying within your budget.

There are also signs that you are not succeeding. For example, you could run out of money in your grocery envelope before your next paycheck. When this happens it could pay to track your spending in that area a bit more closely to make sure you aren't overspending. Maybe you should buy more veggies and fewer meats to save money.

Chapter 17: Clear Your Debts Fast!

After you feel that you have sufficient capabilities to manage your home's finances on your own, the first thing you need to work on is your debts. Only after you have eliminated your debts can you add to your savings positively. This was the most challenging task for me. With the easy availability of home loans, car loans, education loans, personal loans and the credit card, we sunk into deep debts. By the time I realized it, I knew it was time to act towards it rather than sinking more into it. Better late than never.

A haphazard and unorganized debt payment was doing us no good. Therefore, I decided to take up a step-by-step approach. Repaying all debts became my prime concern. Let us gradually go through effective measures that you could take as well.

1) **Say no to debts** - Any more debt is a strict 'NO'. We cannot continue to add on to what we already have.

2) **Stop using the credit card** - This is the main culprit that ruins many homes. Cut it up in half. If at all you desperately need it, keep no more than one only for emergency. No matter how much we argue in its favour, it eventually leads to increased debts.

3) **Make a debt chart** - We need to have a plan. I made a list of all the debts that I owed. The next step was to chalk down the repayment plan. I calculated the minimum monthly payment I need to make to clear my debts within a year. This can be flexible according to your debts, expenses and income. However, remain focused on your target and timeline.

Next, I decided to repay the smaller debts first. You may consider the terms of your debt and prioritize your debts accordingly.

4) **Record your spending** - We have discussed it under the budget making plan. Recording would help you analyze where you can curb unnecessary expenses. It is the small expenses, which add up to go beyond what you earn.

5) **Live frugally** - Hard as it may sound, if you seriously want to eliminate your debts, you have to live frugally until your debts are paid. Only when your expenses are less, will you have ample to pay off your debts. Careful planning of necessities and purchase is needed. Had I not lived frugally, I would have never managed to clear off all loans. I discontinued my gym membership and took up running, walked down to nearby destinations rather than travel by car, took to public transport more often, did not host guests for a year, reduced my intake of coffee etc. Minute compromises add up to large savings overtime.

6) **Eliminate unnecessary expenses** - Things that we do not direly need at the moment can be eliminated. Example cable

TV, shopping for new clothes unless required, kitty parties, expensive cosmetics etc. We need to make a list of only necessary items and eliminate every other item that can be postponed for a future date.

7) **Keep debt as your first bill** - As soon as you get your income, repay the targeted amount for the month. Do not commit the mistake of repaying debt out of the money that remains after the monthly expenses. Shrug off a certain amount as savings after that for emergencies and with the remaining amount, budget your monthly expense.

8) **Increase your income** - Though your husband is the sole provider, a dual source of income might help in resolving your debts sooner. It may be any small skill of yours using which you can work part-time from home. I started freelancing from home. You may take tuitions at home, bake and sell, write columns for magazines etc.

9) **Look for alternatives and bulk discounts** - When you shop for groceries, make a list and stick to it. Buy cheaper alternatives and buy groceries in bulk. Buying in bulk helps, you buy them at a cheaper cost than buying the same quantity in installments. Focus on nutrition and cut down on junks.

10) **Celebrate success** - It is important to keep motivated. A low expense lifestyle can become despairing over the time. Whenever you accomplish a target, go out and celebrate with your family. This will make you look forward to complete your targets.

This is a ten-point solution for you to clear debts fast and efficiently. Once your debts are clear, you may focus on investments and growth.

Chapter 18: Casting The Net

The next steps are sometimes "painful". This is because they force us to face, and "swallow" our actual spending decisions and compare these with what we had budgeted for in the previous chapter. Of all the steps, this takes the most discipline, attention to detail, and commitment, if you want to make this whole budgeting process work. You have spent a good deal of time to plan, and now you have to deliver on the plan. Remember, "For a plan to work, you have to work the plan."

When I say, "cast the net," I mean that you have to "catch" or capture all the financial transactions, especially spending. You need to do this on a regular and consistent basis. This is part of financial discipline, and financial discipline means financial freedom.

First, you have to physically organize your receipts properly. I suggest getting an accordion file, which has several pockets where you can drop in your receipts as you collect them. At the end of each day, take all the receipts that you accumulated and file them accordingly.

Next, you have to record these transactions. There is a multitude of ways that this can be accomplished with today's technology.

Useful technology that's come out in the last ten years are desktop scanners. When you feed your documents for scanning, the machine's software helps categorize the documents and saves an image of the document to an electronic file that you can upload to a computer.

Even without a scanner, you can still use the spreadsheet we've provided to input and monitor your expenses.

If you'd prefer a different budgeting spreadsheet, you can use **Microsoft Excel,** which has dozens of budgeting templates. The beauty of using the templates provided by **Excel** is that they not only provide you with a means to input your actual expenses, you can also initially create your original budget within the template, and compare your actual expenses.

For the increasing number of people whose lives center around tablets and cell phones, not only are there **Excel** versions for both **Android**-based and **IOS** (Apple) phones and tablets, but these mobile platforms have their own proprietary spreadsheet applications as well. The best part is that these "apps" are usually free, and can be downloaded from **Google Play** or **Apple'**s app store.

Because they're so portable, your phone or tablet is an excellent tool for budgeting. You can update your expenses and check up on your financial progress anytime and anywhere. Even better, there are free apps that you can download. On **Android** phones, for example, there are 4 stars plus rated apps like **Spending Tracker, Expense Manager,** and **Good**

166

budget. There are IOS versions of these in the **Apple** app store, together with apps created specifically for **iPhone** and **iPad.**

If you plan to incorporate your budgeting escapades with the financial planning of your new found wealth as a result of your savings, you can use **Quicken** © which started out ages ago as a checkbook program, and has been transformed into so-called debt management and investment tracking software. It costs anywhere from $30 to $100 depending on the features you want and can be used on both **Windows** and **Mac**. Of course, **Quicken** can be used on phones and tablets, but is designed primarily to "sync" with the primary **Quicken** software.

Regardless of what application or software you use, remember that the key to your budgeting success is **commitment** and **consistency**. Get all the tools you can get your hands on to allow you to be comfortable with the process. However, you must remember to set aside a time each day, or at worse, a few times a week, to record your expenses and track them compared to what you have budgeted for yourself. If you do this, you are on the road to financial freedom and independence!

Once again, be consistent and most important of all; don't get discouraged if you overspend on an item. After all, feeling uncomfortable about living beyond your means is a welcome development!

Chapter 19: Easy Supermarket Bargain Shopping Tips

Supermarkets are notorious for syphoning out every penny they can out of us. Remember those mental cues we talked about in an earlier chapter; supermarkets are notorious for using these extensively. Some of the tricks used by supermarkets include:

*Placing sweets and magazines closer to the till: Most items placed nearest to the till are often times impulse buys aimed at giving the store a last chance to milk your pocket.

*Store layouts that force you to walk through the whole supermarket before getting to your desired items: Most supermarkets will space fast moving and regularly bought goods across the supermarket floor. Then they line up the space between the till and your desired item with eye-catching goods that spell-out "buy me".

*Placing their most profitable items at eye level: This is ok, but a point to note is that most goods profitable to the store are often times not a bargain.

By informing yourself about some of the tricks they use, you can guard yourself against what I will call "Targeted profit making bargains." To help you out, I have also compiled a list of a few things you can do to ensure value for money when shopping at a supermarket.

1: The downshift challenge

This sounds like something you would expect to hear at a racetrack competition. However, it features in our bargain hunting and money saving lessons. To get started on the downshift challenge, walk into your favorite supermarket and instead of picking your favorite brand item, drop one level. If you cannot tell the difference between your brand and the alternative brand, you are better of using the cheaper brand.

2: Shopping while hungry is a no

Research shows that if you shop at a supermarket while hungry, you are more prone to buying items you do not necessarily require in the hope that it will quench your hunger pangs. Additionally, you should be fearfully aware of pick-up shops. This means that if you have to restock an item in the middle of the week, say for instance milk, you should not pick up a basket because chances are, once you pick up that basket, you will fill it.

3: Again...compare your trolley cost

Comparing will come up many of times throughout bargain hunting. To compare your trolley cost with that of other major stores, you can use MySupermarket. MySupermarket compares your supermarket trolley items with all the major stores such as Tesco, Sainsbury's etc. Using this method can easily save money by buying at a store that has a cheaper trolley value for your goods. The fun thing about using MySupermarket is that it offers you cheaper options as you enter your data and thus offering cheaper same value items. In addition, the platform is available for your Android and IOS smartphone.

4: Track the value of the bargain

Earlier on, I hinted at the fact that supermarkets are notorious for employing any trick to milk your pocket; this includes listing "on offer" items as cheap while they are in fact not. The untold trick to avoiding this is to differentiate between promos and the awesome bargain offers. Luckily, the application above (MySupermarket) now has a comparison feature to it that charts products price and its history. This helps the consumer learn if the store price is feasible and realistic. To do this, you simply need to sign up or login to the platform and search for an item. When the product page loads, scroll down the page to get to the average price chart for your item. I can guarantee that the result displayed will surprise you immensely.

You can also set up price alerts on goods you buy regularly. This is especially useful when you want to get a bargain on your favorite goods such as groceries. Using the same MySupermarket app or platform, all you need to do is search for the item you want and click on the add price alert option. The platform will send you an alert when the price of the item falls in any of the major stores. If you do not use a smartphone app, the platform also offers a very nifty browser plug-in.

Chapter 20: Write Down Your Priorities

From the same worksheet that you used to write down your goals (Goal Saving Worksheet), you will need to determine and write down which goals are most important to you.

How to write down your priorities.

Remember the lesson you learned in Determine Your Need & Want, it's crucial for that part. Let me show you how to write down your priorities:

Determine if one of these goals needs to be accomplished before a certain date. If you need to buy new equipment or do some renovations 3 months from now, you should probably make it a priority. Determine where you can make cuts to save more money today, so you will have enough in 3 months. Remember, the sooner you start saving, the better.

Put them in a chronological order. Place the more important goals that you wish to accomplish first at the top of the list. What is first on the list must be done first. You need to respect the decision you make today for the next couple of months. Make sure that what is first, second and third are important goals for your budget. Do not look at your wants on this list, especially if you have something that is a necessity in your life.

Set a target date. When does it need to be done? Take a step back and analyze your current situation. If it can wait, put the target date for that in the long-term category. For the ones that need to be done sooner, they should take first priority.

Calculate how much it costs. Determine the costs for each goal so that you can know how much money you need to accomplish these goals. TIP: always put aside more than you need, in case it costs a bit more than you had anticipated.

Decide how much will you save per month for each goal. Based on the funds you have available, you are free to determine how much you want to give for each goal. The higher priorities should have more than the lower ones.

Once you have established your goals, the next step is to prioritize the most urgent/important ones. This is beneficial to make sure that our money goes where our priorities are.

All it really takes is few minutes of your time, and some good old-fashioned self-control. Once you decided how much to save for each goal and what is more important now, you need to be your own coach for your future expenses and investments. You can't expect your budget to be successful at the end if you cheat.

When is it necessary?

The point of writing down your priorities is that when you are willing to waste money, you are going to think twice before you do it because you know it doesn't align with your priorities. This is what you want!

What does it mean to entrepreneurs?

For entrepreneurs, this is as important as identifying which tasks need to be done first. If you don't have a to-do list, I recommend you keeping one updated daily. Having your business goals written down along with their priority level helps you quickly know what your focus needs to be. When you have multiples employees, you want most of them focusing on what needs to be done today and some of them on what needs to be done tomorrow.

If you are running a startup, or you are self-employed, it means to do what is required to be done today. Are you doing to do an open house a week before its schedule? Obviously not. Same goes for your goals. Write them down and identify which ones are a priority. This way, your money will go where it needs to go.

One of the best tips that I can give is this one: **always keep your check balance empty**. You are not supposed to have any leftovers in there! If you do, put it somewhere else where a little extra can help. In your budget, you should already have something set aside for leisurely activities, otherwise you will get burnt out.

The sooner you establish what needs to be done first, the faster you can start saving and building the funds necessary to make it. I can't identify for you what you need to invest in, but an investment should help your business to grow. If it doesn't, it might not be an investment. **Watch where your money goes and you will see yourself finding new goals constantly.**

Here are the benefits of writing down your priorities:

Your money goes where you want it to go. By writing down your priorities, you decide where your extra money after paying all your bills goes. No more wasted money on stuff you don't care. Your **hard**

worked money goes where it matters! If you have a wife, trust me, she will be happy that the projects you've been talking for years are finally happening.

You make progress. You will no longer wonder how you've been working for years and yet you aren't progressing. Indeed, when you set goals, when you prioritized them and you make plan to achieve them, **they are most likely to happen.** One goal after the other, you make progress. Either these are your life goals or your business goals to create a great company, you are moving forward. I get exited just to think about it!

You identify what is important to you. "I know what's important for me, Jean-Gabriel!" Yes, but why your money doesn't represent it? By identifying them, you give yourself the chance to respect what you truly want. It only takes few minutes, but the consequences are huge. Do what is necessary and you will experience new aspects of life.

You become more organized. Your goals are like your to-do list, but more exiting! You become organized with what you want to accomplish in life or in business and when. Failing to plan is planning to fail. Whenever you have a new idea or a goal you would like to reach, you will immediately **write it down** and set it as a priority for when it needs to be done. It changes how you live and since you do more, you feel better. That's always the goal.

Chapter 21: Resources To Help Save Time And Money

Finding ways to save money can be difficult, especially if you haven't done so in the past. People might be giving you all sorts of advice, but you don't know where to begin. If you feel threatened by the idea of changing your habits to save time and money, then you're not the only one! It takes time and knowledge about how you can change existing habits. The great thing about the internet is that it is a wonderful resource for people experiencing our same situation. Let's take a look at some resources that we can use to save money so that we can experience personal wealth.

Store websites

Store websites are always up to date on what that particular store is offering for sale that week. It also gives the regular prices of the items so that you know what to expect to spend when it's not on sale. If you're thinking about making a large purchase, comparing store websites on the item might ultimately save you a ton of money!

Newspaper ads

Newspaper ads are the older way of getting the word out that there is a sale in progress. You may not think to check the store website, but seeing the ads in the newspaper might spark your interest in what you want to buy and give you ideas. Use this as a resource when it comes to grocery shopping. The grocery stores advertise their sales in the newspaper frequently!

Coupon websites

Coupon websites are a good way of finding which store and manufacturer coupons are out there at the moment. Make sure that you are using a reliable coupon website, as there are a lot of fraudulent coupons out there. Try websites such as coupons.com and couponsuzy.com. These sites both give you the same coupons that you will find in the newspapers that you can print out and use!

Price comparison apps

In the age of smartphones, there are numerous apps that will allow you to compare prices on just about everything out there. If you're going to get gas, there's an app that tells you which of the closer gas stations has the best price. By using your apps, you can find the best price on just about everything you wish to buy!

Financial advisors

Financial advisors are becoming more prevalent in our society. You don't have to pay big bucks to benefit from their advice. Simply jump on the internet and read articles in online publications written by trusted financial advisors. By using your resources, you are learning to save money while actually saving money!

Coupon cards

Many of the grocery stores out there offer discount and coupon cards. There are also coupon cards that can be bought from school fundraisers that will save you money. When confronted with the decision as to own either of these, it's a good idea and usually will save you more money that you would spend to obtain the card in the first place. Also, store cards are usually free!

Comparison shopping online

By taking the time to compare your intended purchase between different retailers and different brands, you can get the best product at the best price. While this might be a little more time consuming than just going to the store and buying it, it will save you hard earned money!

Don't be afraid to use your resources in order to get the best prices out there. There are tons of ways to make sure that you're not spending more than you should on something. You might invest more time preparing to buy it, but this also gives you the chance to think through the purchase before jumping in and it gives you the opportunity to buy it as inexpensively as you can!

Chapter 22: How To Set A Realistic Savings Target

If you're always at zero at the end of the month, you're obviously doing something wrong. No matter what life situation you are in, you should always be able to put at least **20 percent** of your salary aside. This is your goal if you are in debt at the moment or your account balance is less than 10'000. You're going to put 20 % of your income aside every month, no matter how much you earn. Now you can already calculate how much money this will bring you in 5 months. Even if it doesn't look like much, it's worth going through with it for the next two years. Because, as already mentioned, once you have a certain amount saved up, the money starts "having children".

If you're already good at saving, you can increase your savings rate by up to 50%. See what is possible for you. The more you save, the faster your wealth will grow.

If that's still too slow for you, you can make sure to create additional streams of income. We will also look at this topic in this book.

But back to your vision board. Design it and write down your fortune as a number that you want to reach on a certain date in the next two years. For example, 150'000 on July 31, 2022.

How to lower your expenses

The most important thing in order to get a better savings rate is to know what you're spending your money on in the first place. For this, I highly recommend using a budget app. I use **AndroMoney**. There, I can enter my income and expenses and nice charts show me what I spend my money on.

You just have to get used to entering each expense individually. Use categories such as snacks, dining out, groceries, rent, public transport, car, your hobbies, alcohol, travel, gifts, medical expenses, medicine, clothes, etc.

If you have an overview of your expenses, you can focus on the details you need to change to save money. As an advanced step, you can then create a budget plan that allows you to spend money in a relaxed way every month, and at the end of the month your calculations should work out.

Money sucking categories and how to minimize these expenses

Now let's take a look at some of these money-sucking categories and get tips on how to reduce spending in those categories. You probably can't focus on everything at the same time, otherwise, it's a little overwhelming. That's why you'll find a checklist of budget targets at the end of the chapter. Write a budget target per category for your monthly expenses and gradually focus on more categories. When you reach your budget goal, you can tick it off. You can also copy the list and hang it on your door or next to the Vision Board.

Alcohol and going out

If alcohol is a big cost for you, it would be beneficial to drastically reduce alcohol consumption. Above all: don't drink in bars or restaurants anymore. Drinks in bars and restaurants literally pull the money out of your pocket. Then, there is also a tip and perhaps you have to invite your friends from time to time. No! With good friends, you don't have to. Tell them about your savings goal and, if necessary, allow yourself a monthly budget that you can use for drinking outside of your apartment. Don't exceed that budget. Of course, it would be even better if you only enjoy drinks at home and buy alcohol in the cheapest shop you find. You can have friends over at home as well. Make sure that you have some good music on and perhaps everyone can bring something to eat (or drink). This way, you save the money for the expensive club.

Snacks between meals

The daily temptations of snacks are huge. A chocolate bar that goes with your bread bun (although the bun or croissant is probably too expensive if you buy one every day, so, perhaps bake it yourself or limit it to once a week) a doughnut with your coffee, a bag of chips in the evening, etc. If you are tempted to snack, you need a big dose of self-discipline from now on. Don't buy anything at a kiosk or in restaurants! It is best to avoid snacks and only eat at the main meals. According to interval fasting, you would also do something for your health. However, if that sounds too hard, at least buy your snacks at discount stores, and then take them with you. No spontaneous purchases on the go! For example, if you always eat the same chocolate bars, buy them in a large pack, as they are usually cheaper and take the amount you need with you every day.

Coffee

If you're a coffee lover who drinks five cups or more a day, or you need your Starbucks cappuccino every morning, a decent amount can add up throughout the year. Calculate this amount. If you're a Starbucks follower, as hard as it sounds, you should scale back your consumption and reward yourself with a Starbucks coffee at most once a month. In the office, you may be lucky, and the coffee is free or only costs little.

However, if you buy the coffee on the go, you should consider buying a cheap machine for at home. For Starbucks coffees, you need a milk frother and possibly a caramel syrup. So, you can prepare your coffee at home. You could also bring the coffee for the day in a thermos.

Even coffee dates with friends can be moved home if you have a good machine.

Conclusion

This book clearly outlines the potency of compound saving and investing. It is a shame that young people fail to harness it as early in life as is possible.

Here is the thing; you could do something else with your money; you could shun stocks, bonds, the stock market, real estate, and everything else. However, if you allow the compound effect to have an effect on your money, you would still be able to retire comfortably.

Thank you and good luck!